Grammar Activities

Grammar Activities 2

Upper intermediate

Will Forsyth
Sue Lavender

Heinemann English Language Teaching
A division of Reed Educational and Professional Publishing Limited
Halley Court, Jordan Hill, Oxford OX2 8EJ
OXFORD MADRID FLORENCE ATHENS PRAGUE SAO PAULO MEXICO CITY
CHICAGO PORTSMOUTH (NH) TOKYO SINGAPORE KUALA LUMPUR
MELBOURNE AUCKLAND JOHANNESBURG IBADAN GABORONE

ISBN 0 435 25095 7

Text © Will Forsyth, Sue Lavender 1995

Design and illustration © Heinemann Publishers (Oxford) Ltd 1995

First published 1995

For John Lavender, to remember you always

Permission to copy

The material in this book is copyright. However, the publisher grants permission for copies of pages to be made without fee on those pages marked with the PHOTOCOPIABLE symbol.

Private purchasers may make copies for their own use or for use by classes of which they are in charge; school purchasers may make copies for use within and by the staff and students of the school only. This permission does not extend to additional schools or branches of an institution, who should purchase a separate master copy of the book for their own use.

For copying in any other circumstances, prior permission in writing must be obtained from Heinemann Publishers (Oxford) Ltd.

Designed by Portfolio Design Consultancy

Cover design by Stafford & Stafford

Illustrated by: Belinda Evans, Frank James, Satoshi Kambayashi, Mike Mosedale, Shaun Williams

Printed in Great Britain by Thomson Litho, East Kilbride, Scotland
Bound by Hunter and Foulis, Edinburgh, Scotland
96 97 98 10 9 8 7 6 5 4 3 2

Contents

1 Notes to the teacher
2 Adverbs of time 1
3 Adverbs of time 2
4 Adverbs of time 3
5 Adverbs of time 4
6 Advice and suggestions 1
7 Advice and suggestions 2
8 Articles 1
9 Articles 2
10 Articles and countable and uncountable nouns
11 Countable and uncountable 1
12 Countable and uncountable 2
13 Countable and uncountable 3
14 Enough and plenty
15 Futures 1   *future perfect and future perfect continuous*
16 Futures 2   *future perfect and future perfect continuous*
17 Futures 3   *mixed futures*
18 If sentences 1
19 If sentences 2
20 If sentences 3   *mixed if sentences*
21 Indirect questions 1
22 Indirect questions 22
23 Infinitive and gerund 1
24 Infinitive and gerund 2
25 Infinitive and gerund 3
26 Infinitive and gerund 4
27 Linking words 1   *unless, as long as, in case, although*
28 Linking words 2   *although, in spite of, despite, because, however, due to, therefore*
29 Linking words 3   *although, in spite of, despite, because, however, due to, therefore*
30 Look, look like, look as if 1
31 Look, look like, look as if 2
32 Modal verbs 1
33 Modal verbs 2
34 Modal verbs 3
35 Modal verbs 4
36 Modal verbs 5   *would/should/could have done referring to the past*
37 Modal verbs 6   *would/should/could have done referring to the present and future*
38 Modal verbs 7
39 Modal verbs 8   *must, might, could and can't for deduction*
40 Modal verbs 9   *must, might, could and can't for deduction*
41 Modal verbs 10   *could, be able to and manage to*
42 Modal verbs 11   *could, be able to and manage to*
43 Passives 1
44 Passives 2
45 Passives 3
46 Passives 4

47	Past and present	
48	Pasts 1	past and past perfect, simple and continuous
49	Pasts 2	
50	Pasts 3	
51	Pasts 4	
52	Prepositions 1	
53	Prepositions 2	
54	Present perfect and past simple 1	
55	Present perfect and past simple 2	
56	Relative clauses 1	defining relative clauses
57	Relative clauses 2	defining and non-defining relative clauses
58	Relative clauses 3	defining and non-defining relative clauses
59	Relative clauses 4	mixed relative clauses
60	Reporting 1	
61	Reporting 2	
62	Simple and continuous 1	senses and actions
63	Simple and continuous 2	senses and actions
64	Simple and continuous 3	states and actions
65	Simple and continuous 4	states and actions
66	So and such 1	
67	So and such 2	
68	Subject and object questions 1	
69	Subject and object questions 2	
70	Substitution words 1	
71	Substitution words 2	
72	Used to 1	*used to do* and *get used to doing*
73	Used to 2	*used to do* and *get used to doing*
74	Wish 1	*wish* + *could*, simple past and past perfect
75	Wish 2	*wish* + simple past, past perfect, *would*
76	Wish 3	states and actions
	Review 1	
	Review 2	
	Review 3	
	Review 4	
	Review 5	
Answer key	Page 82	
Index	Page 91	
Questionnaire	Page 92	

Notes to the teacher

Grammar Activities 2 is for students at an upper-intermediate level including those just preparing for the Cambridge First Certificate examination. It is intended as a coursebook supplement. It provides presentation and consolidation, using a variety of contexts and approaches, of grammatical areas which cause learners problems at this level. It contains 75 free-standing worksheets arranged alphabetically by grammar point and five review worksheets. Where there are several worksheets that focus on the same grammatical area, they are ordered from simple to complex so they can be used independently or in sequence.

There are two main types of worksheet: *contextualised worksheets* and *problem-solving worksheets*. The contextualised worksheets provide a story, situation or game which gives the learners the opportunity to practise using the structure in an appropriate context. The problem-solving worksheets take a cognitive approach. They provide activities that help the learners arrive at a fuller understanding of the meanings, formation and rules of the use of the structure. They are identified by this symbol: ▼

Using Grammar Activities 2 in class

We use grammar activities both for grammar presentations, whether fresh or remedial, and for quick review activities. When using a worksheet for presentation, before giving out the exercise, we start by introducing the topic or situation, we build up the language together with the class, and finally we give the exercise out for written consolidation. The topic or situation can be introduced in a number of ways: by drawing the picture on the board or showing the picture(s) around the class; by writing key words on the board; or simply by describing the situation. To build up the language we ask questions about the picture(s) to establish who is involved, what they are doing, and what they might be saying, or what is being said about them. We invite as many class suggestions and ideas as possible, correcting the learners' use of the structure where necessary. When everyone has had the chance to hear everyone else's ideas, the class can practise the structure. They do this by pretending to be the people in the picture(s) or by remembering what the class has said. Finally, we give out copies of the exercise for the class to fill in from memory.

We use the problem-solving activities with classes that have already used the structure in a limited context and could benefit from thinking about it more widely and more intensively. We do this some time after the initial presentation, usually on a different day, or with a class that needs review only. We give the class one or two examples of the structure and ask for ideas on how it is different from a similar structure, (for example, *could/would, used to/be used to, look like/look as if*, etc.) or if they can spot mistakes in it. The answers can lead to a short discussion of what the structure means and how it is used. We then give out copies of the exercise for the learners to discuss and complete in groups.

Either the contextualised or the problem-solving exercises can be used for quick review as a five- or ten-minute activity at the beginning or end of a class. This not only reviews the structure, but is also a good way of breaking up the lesson and changing pace.

The last five *Review worksheets* are intended as review or diagnostic units. Each one contains exercises on a variety of structures that are covered more thoroughly elsewhere in the book.

We hope that both you and your students enjoy using this book and that it also gives you ideas for exercises of your own.

2 Adverbs of time 1

A A friend asks you some questions. Read your thoughts and then answer your friend using the word given in brackets.

What your friend asks:	Your thoughts:	What you say:
Example: Would you like to see 'Dusty Moonlight'?	You saw it last night.	Actually, _I've already seen it._ (already)
1 Did you enjoy the book I lent you?	The book is unread.	I'm afraid _____ (yet)
2 Have you rung Jane?	You know you promised to do this last week but there hasn't been time.	I'm sorry but _____ (still)
3 How long have you had that shirt?	You bought it when you went to India.	I've _____ (since)
4 Do you know Steve's coming round this evening?	This will be the first time you've met him.	I don't think I _____ (ever)
5 Would you like to borrow this novel?	You've read it before.	Thanks, but to tell you the truth I've _____ (already)
6 Shall we go to an Indian restaurant tonight?	It will be your first visit to an Indian restaurant.	That'll be exciting, I _____ (never)
7 Have I seen that hat before?	You got it six months ago.	Yes, I think so, I _____ (for)
8 How can I work out all these figures on my own?	You think it would be a good idea to buy a computer.	Have you _____ (ever)?

B Use the words in the box to complete the adverts.

> still   already   yet

1 If you haven't applied for your free gift, _____ this is your last chance!

2 _____ writing letters the old-fashioned way? Send for our word-processing brochure **TODAY!**

3 BUY YOUR LOTTERY TICKET TODAY; 500 LUCKY WINNERS _____ !

PHOTOCOPIABLE

© Will Forsyth, Sue Lavender 1995. Published by Heinemann English Language Teaching. This sheet may be photocopied and used within the class.

Adverbs of time 2   3

A Rewrite the following sentences to include the word in brackets.

Example:
I haven't been to Australia.   (ever)   I haven't ever been to Australia.

1 I've been to Australia.   (already) _____
2 I haven't been to Australia.   (yet) _____
3 Have you been to Australia? (ever) _____
4 I've been to Australia.   (never) _____
5 I haven't been to Australia.   (still) _____
6 Australia is the most beautiful country I've seen.   (ever) _____

B Here are some possible continuations of the sentences in A. Write the letter of the most appropriate continuation next to the number of each sentence.

Example: __b__ 1 ____ 2 ____ 3 ____ 4 ____ 5 ____ 6 ____

a) so I strongly recommend it for a holiday.

b) and I have no special plans to go there.

c) so I'd like to go somewhere different this year.

d) I can't remember if you've told me.

e) and I have no special plans to go there.

f) but I hope to go one day soon.

g) although I've been trying to go for a long time.

C Choose the *most appropriate* word to add to each sentence and then write the sentence with the word in the correct place.

Example:
I've been to Paris; I was there last year.   yet/(already)
I've already been to Paris; I was there last year.

1 It's the most beautiful picture I've seen.   never/ever
_____

2 I haven't been to Germany, but I'd like to go one day.   never/ever
_____

3 You were talking about going to Munich; have you been there?   ever/yet
_____

4 I'm trying to find someone who knows about Canada; have you been there?   ever/yet
_____

5 Although Mongolia has opened its borders, it's difficult to fly there.   still/yet
_____

6 We haven't visited Padua, but we plan to go in the spring.   yet/already
_____

4 Adverbs of time 3

A Decide which of the words in brackets completes each of the sentences. Put the correct word into the puzzle to discover the word hidden in the centre of the puzzle.

1 I haven't _____ been here. (never/often)
2 _____ I arrived in Britain I haven't felt homesick. (since/while)
3 I think I've been there _____ . (never/twice)
4 We first met six years _____ . (now/ago)
5 I've _____ realised what you said. (just/ever)
6 I _____ used to come here and sit by the river. (yesterday/sometimes)
7 I promise to meet you _____ the end of the day. (before/during)
8 I _____ saw a play by Shakespeare. (ever/once)
9 By the age of twenty he had _____ finished university. (usually/already)
10 I'm afraid I'll be busy _____ six o'clock. (since/until)
11 I _____ see you these days. (weekly/rarely)
12 I'm sorry but I haven't had time to do it _____ . (now/yet)

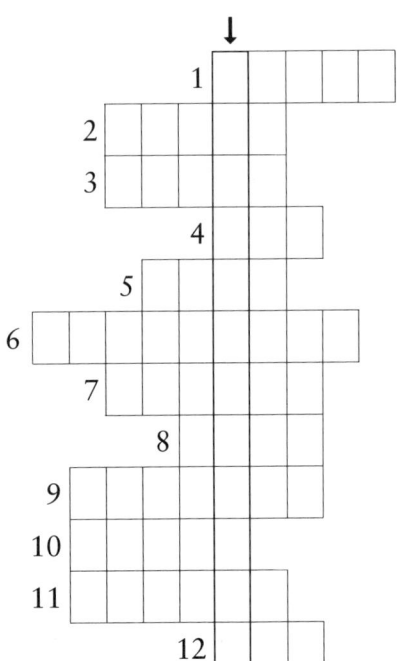

B Match each item in column A with one in column B to make an expression which will complete one of the sentences on the right.

A	B	Example: I used to know him quite well, but I
i) almost	a) ago	<u>almost never</u> see him these days.
ii) long	b) now	1 I'm sure I saw Mick _____ so he can't be far away.
iii) just	c) ever	2 It happened _____ and before anyone can remember.
iv) never	d) never	3 She told her children they must _____ take sweets from strangers.

Adverbs of time 4

A A tennis champion is talking about his friend, Ted. Fill in the missing words and then put them in the puzzle to discover who Ted is.

1. Ted and I first met about three years _____ .
2. That was _____ we both lived in London.
3. We've been working together _____ that time.
4. I've _____ worked so closely with anyone else.
5. We haven't _____ had an argument.
6. And we certainly haven't got tired of each other _____ .

Example: In fact we've __already__ had quite a lot of success.

7. I hope we can continue our partnership _____ many years to come.
8. _____ we go on working together I know things will go well.
9. I'm sure I _____ have a lot to learn from Ted.

Example: A L R E A D Y

B Philip and Jenny meet in Oxford. They haven't seen each other for a long time. Complete their conversation using the phrases in the box.

> (nowadays) sooner or later ago whenever over these days
> present ages during moment long time every now and then

Philip: Where are you living __nowadays__, Jenny?
Jenny: Well, I've been in Oxford 1 _____ the last six months.
Philip: Really? So when did you leave London?
Jenny: London? Oh, I left about five years 2 _____ .
Philip: And how 3 _____ do you think you'll stay in Oxford?
Jenny: Well, I'm quite happy at the 4 _____ , but I suppose 5 _____ I'll want to go back to London again.
Philip: Are you still in touch with Paul and Sharon?
Jenny: Yes, I see Paul 6 _____ ; in fact 7 _____ he comes to Oxford but I haven't heard from Sharon for 8 _____ .
Philip: So who are you working for 9 _____ ?
Jenny: Well, I've been unemployed for a 10 _____ ; in fact I'm looking for a job at 11 _____ .
Philip: I'm sorry to hear that. Why don't you come over for a weekend soon?
Jenny: Yes, I'd love to; in fact it looks as if I'll have plenty of free time 12 _____ the autumn.

6 Advice and suggestions 1

A Richa has made eight suggestions about your stay in Britain. Use one item from each box each time to find out what they are.

| Maybe you should
Why don't you
I think you'd better
How about
If I were you I'd
You could always
Have you thought
Why not
Perhaps you ought | visiting Wales
of staying in a bed and breakfast
rent a car
to come and stay with me | .
?|

Example: ___Maybe you should rent a car.___

B Richa is telling you about some problems she has. Complete your advice to her by choosing the appropriate picture and using the verb given.

    buy   look   have   take

    use   borrow   have   take

Richa's problem
Example: I have a bad headache today.
1 The bus is really expensive!

2 This cassette player sounds terrible!
3 I find it really difficult to see the TV.
4 There are so many words in this book that I don't know!
5 I can't afford the hotel prices.
6 I don't eat meat.
7 I feel cold.

Your advice
Perhaps you should ___take some asprin.___
Well, have you thought _____
_____
Why not _____
Maybe you ought _____
_____
Well, you could always _____
_____
Why don't _____
How about _____
You'd better _____

Advice and suggestions 2

A Look at the pictures and comments and choose the most appropriate reply, *a* or *b.*

1

a) You ought to be wearing a seat belt.
b) If I were you, I'd be wearing a seat belt.

2

a) Yes, you could always have it out today.
b) Yes, you'd better have it out today.

3

a) You'd better try painting it green.
b) Why don't you try painting it green?

4

a) Quick, you'd better get a cloth!
b) Quick, have you thought of getting a cloth?

5

a) You should get it repaired over there.
b) How about getting it repaired over there?

6

a) Yes, why not take the medicine twice a day before meals?
b) Yes, you should take the medicine twice a day before meals.

B Match the correct replies in A with their meanings. Note that a reply may match more than one meaning.

a) The speaker is giving professional advice. __1a__ ____ ____

b) The speaker is giving advice as a friend or equal. ____ ____ ____

c) The speaker is suggesting only one of a number of possible courses of action. ____ ____

d) The speaker is strongly suggesting one immediate action as the only possibility. ____ ____

8 Articles 1

A Complete the conversation by putting the words in the box in the correct place. With each word, add *a* or *the* if necessary.

> life   children   violent film   (good film)   film   film
> films   violence   violence   violent films   quality

John: I saw ___a good film___ on TV last night.

Jane: Oh? What was it?

John: 'Blood or Money'.

Jane: Was it 1 _____ ?

John: Well, it was quite violent, I suppose.

Jane: I don't like 2 _____ .

John: 3 _____ is a natural part of 4 _____ ; you can't escape from it.

Jane: But that's no reason for enjoying it.

John: Well, it's not 5 _____ I enjoy; it's 6 _____ of 7 _____ that's important.

Jane: So why does it need to be violent, then?

John: It doesn't need to be violent but if you're going to make 8 _____ about something important and real, it will probably be violent too.

Jane: That's rubbish. And anyway, I don't think they should show 9 _____ with violence on television; there might be 10 _____ watching, and I don't think it's good for them.

B Match each sentence with its correct ending, *a*, *b*, or *c*.

1 He loves travelling and learning different   a) language.
2 Humans are differentiated from animals by   b) the language.
3 She decided to leave her job in Romania   c) languages.
   because she couldn't learn

4 Wearing seat-belts saves   a) lives.
5 Before her death she seemed to lose interest in   b) the life.
6 He gave up his office job as he didn't like   c) life.

C Risto has written an essay about unemployment. Here is the first paragraph. There are ten mistakes with articles (there are no mistakes with singular or plural nouns). Find the mistakes and correct them.

>   The unemployment is one of a most important problems in a world today. It affects all countries: not only South America, Africa and Asia, but also the Europe and United States too. And it is not just the modern problem either; it has been with us for the centuries. The unemployment destroys the people's lives, it breaks up family and it makes society poor. The question is; what can we do about it?

Articles 2

A Four sentences are true and two are false. Put ticks ✓ against the true ones.

1 You can use *a* with plural nouns, for example, *Can you hear a dogs barking?* ☐
2 You can use *the* with plural nouns, for example, *Can you hear the dogs barking?* ☐
3 You can use no article with plural nouns, for example, *Can you hear dogs barking?* ☐
4 You can use *a* with uncountable nouns, for example, *A water is boiling.* ☐
5 You can use *the* with uncountable nouns, for example, *The water is boiling.* ☐
6 You can use no article with uncountable nouns, for example, *Water boils.* ☐

B Look again at the example sentences in part A. Put the four <u>correct</u> examples into the correct paragraph.

a) Sally is in the kitchen with her young daughter, Claire.
    Claire: Can I make the tea, please, Mummy?
    Sally: Yes, but do be careful. Put some water in the kettle, put some tea in the teapot, and when _____, pour it into the pot very carefully.

b) Sally and Claire are still talking.
    Claire: I don't really understand my science classes at school.
    Sally: Why not? What don't you understand?
    Claire: Well, for example, _____ at 100°C, yes?
    Sally: Yes.
    Claire: Well, why?

c) It is night. Helen and Simon are lost in a forest. They are alone.
    Helen: Where are we?
    Simon: I don't know.
    Helen: Wait, I thought I saw a light over there, and listen, _____ _____

d) José and Carmen live on a farm near a forest. They have three dogs. It is night.
    Carmen: José _____
    José: Yes, there might be something out there. I'll go and have a look.

C Match what you say with what you mean.

You say	You mean
1 Can you hear dogs barking?	a) You expect your listener to know which dogs you are talking about.
2 Can you hear the dogs barking?	b) You do not know which dogs; they are new to you.
3 Water boils at 100°C.	a) You mean water in general.
4 The water's boiling.	b) You mean some particular water.
5 Society isn't fair.	a) You mean a particular society.
6 The society is meeting tonight.	b) You mean human society as a whole.
7 *the*	a) You expect your listener to know which particular one(s) you mean.
8 – (no article)	b) You do not mean any particular one(s).

10 Articles and countable and uncountable nouns

There is one mistake or more in all of these signs and sayings. Correct the mistakes.

Example: Please leave ~~the~~ (a) message after ~~a~~ (the) tone

1. If you need a help, please ask for an assistance
2. Advices Centre
3. Road jobs ahead
4. Collect your luggages here
5. Will all personnel please report to a main office.
6. THE ENGLISH SPOKEN HERE.
7. Please shut a door
8. JOURNEY AGENT
9. A sun rises in an east and sets in a west
10. Please leave a camera at the desk
11. Please turn off a light.
12. If you have the complaint, please ask to see the manager.
13. A foreign money not accepted
14. An End
15. Please ring a bell for a service
16. Take the card; any card

© Will Forsyth, Sue Lavender 1995. Published by Heinemann English Language Teaching. This sheet may be photocopied and used within the class.

Countable and uncountable 1

Use the words in bold to finish each of the three sentences. Be careful: sometimes you have to use *a*, for example *a time*, sometimes you have to make the word plural, for example, *times* and sometimes you have to leave the word as it is, for example *time*.

time
Example:
Has there ever been __a time__ when you've felt happy for no reason at all?

1 Learning anything well takes _____ .

2 There will often be _____ when you don't know what to do.

glass

3 Windows are made of _____ .

4 Would you like _____ of wine?

5 Do you wear _____ ?

light

6 They left _____ on all over the house, but they were still burgled.

7 I've got a cigarette, but I haven't got _____ .

8 _____ travels at about 300 000 km a second.

hope

9 They lost everything except _____ .

10 It was something he had always wanted, but it was _____ he never realised.

11 Different people have different _____ for themselves and their children.

lamb

12 We saw _____ playing with one another in the fields.

13 He's as gentle as _____ .

14 We sell _____ at £2.00 a kilo.

experience

15 I had several frightening _____ on holiday.

16 They want someone with _____ of computers.

17 Visiting the temple at night is _____ you shouldn't miss.

belief

18 Tribal people often have strange _____ .

19 Superstition is _____ we can do without.

20 _____ is the absence of doubt.

© Will Forsyth, Sue Lavender 1995. Published by Heinemann English Language Teaching. This sheet may be photocopied and used within the class.

12 Countable and uncountable 2

A Match each sentence with one of the two pictures, *a* or *b*.

1 'Mummy, can I have a lamb?'

2 'Mummy, can I have some lamb?'

3 'Would you like some more cake?'

4 'Would you like another cake?'

5 'It's technically perfect, but it doesn't have any emotion.'

6 'It's technically perfect, but it doesn't have any emotions.'

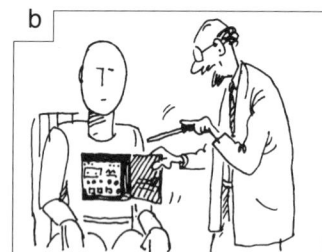

7 'Have you got a spare iron?'

8 'Have you got any spare iron?'

B Some nouns are only countable, for example, *picture* and *oats*. Some nouns are only uncountable, for example, *music* and *wheat*. But many nouns can be either countable or uncountable, depending on the meaning. Match the meanings, forms and examples then finish the example with the correct form of *hair*.

Meaning	Form	Example
Example: The material that something is made of	a) The singular form, for example, *a hair*	i) The detective found three _____ on his shirt.
1 Whole individual items	b) The uncountable form, for example, *hair*	ii) Hairdressers cut and style _____.
2 A whole, individual item	c) The plural form, for example, *hairs*	iii) Wigs are made of **hair**.
3 Something thought of as a mass, not individual items	d) The uncountable form, for example, *hair*	iv) I'm coughing because I've got _____ in my throat.

© Will Forsyth, Sue Lavender 1995. Published by Heinemann English Language Teaching. This sheet may be photocopied and used within the class.

Countable and uncountable 3   13

A The words in the box are the answers to clues 1 to 12. Nine of the words are nearly always uncountable and four are nearly always countable. Write the answers to the clues in the correct column.

> travel   accommodation   secrecy   (research)   sheep   advice
> furniture   people   information   teeth   countryside   work   mice

Example:
It's usually scientific.

1 They chew.
2 It's the opposite of *city*.
3 It includes tents, houses, flats and rooms.
4 Cats chase them.
5 It's the opposite of openness.
6 People love giving it but hate taking it.
7 They live in flocks.
8 It is supposed to broaden the mind.
9 Your home would be empty without it.
10 They are the most dangerous animals on earth.
11 It's at the heart of modern technology.
12 It brings in money.

uncountable	countable
research	

B The words in the box are not really countable or uncountable, but six are always singular and six always plural. Put the words in the correct column.

> the news   the police   scissors   each (of them)   politics   either (of them)
> the poor   both (of them)   everyone   all (of them)   trousers   maths

always singular (_____ is)	always plural (_____ are)

C All these words can be uncountable. Find the five which can also be countable and write *a* or *an* in the box next to the word.

1 [ ] advice   5 [ ] hair   9 [ ] sun
2 [ ] beauty   6 [ ] health   10 [ ] talk
3 [ ] difficulty   7 [ ] icecream   11 [ ] traffic
4 [ ] experience   8 [ ] music   12 [ ] weather

14 Enough and plenty

A Match each sentence with the correct picture, *a* or *b*.

a

1 There are plenty of seats.

2 There are enough seats.

b

B The Hubert family, two adults and four children, want to rent a house in Britain for the summer. They have just visited a house and the estate agent has given them a list of items in the kitchen. Unfortunately, the number of items is not always appropriate. Using the phrases in the box, write the family's comments in the correct place on the list.

(there aren't enough)	there are plenty	there isn't enough
just the right amount	there is plenty	just the right number
there isn't enough	this isn't big enough	these aren't big enough
there aren't quite enough	there are far too many	there aren't enough

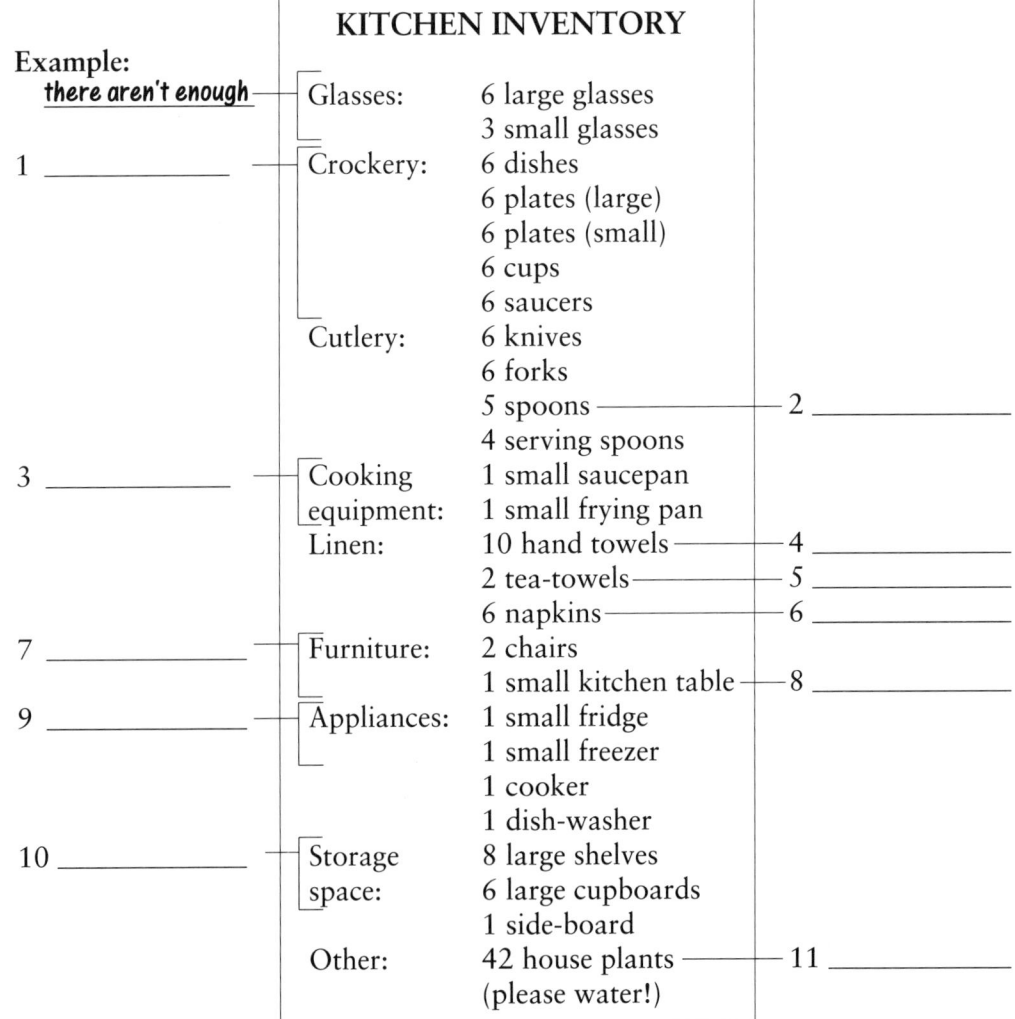

Futures 1

future perfect and future perfect continuous

15

A Use the signs to complete the phrases on the right with the verbs.

BRIDGE CLOSED FOR PAINTING JUNE 10 – 12

'It looks as if it'll be difficult to visit you on the 11th as I've noticed they (example) _will be painting_ the bridge, but the 13th is fine as they 1 _____ _____ the work by then.'

paint
complete

NO ENTRY FINANCE MEETING 14.00 – 16.00

'Can you tell me the decision at lunch-time?' 'Well, I don't think we 2 _____ it by then. We 3 _____ about it in the meeting today.'

take
talk

OFFICE HOURS 9.00 – 1.00   2.00 – 5.00

'Don't come in the morning because I 4 _____ that report, but don't come after 5.00 either because I 5 _____ by then.'

type
leave

☞ Australia welcomes you!

'The sun 6 _____ when we sail into Sydney Harbour, and we 7 _____ Europe forever!'

shine
leave

World population in decline!

'This means that in ten years the population 8 _____ , and in 200 years it 9 _____ below today's levels!'

decline
fall

B Doug has been offered a job with an international magazine. He has heard that the magazine has problems. Doug telephones the editor and makes these comments:

Example: 'I hear you produce only 1000 copies a week.'
1 'I hear you haven't moved to your new offices yet.'
2 'I've been told you sell to only four countries.'
3 'You don't have a computer network system.'
4 'Someone told me you don't have a marketing manager.'
5 'I hear salaries are very low.'
6 'I've heard you have problems with your printing press.'
7 'They tell me you only print in black and white.'

The editor wants Doug to work for the magazine so he answers Doug's worries. Complete the editor's replies using a verb from the box each time.

| sell   raise   solve   (produce)   install   print   move   appoint |

Example: We _will be producing_ at least 10 000 copies a week.
1 We _____ to our new offices.
2 We _____ to at least twelve countries.
3 We _____ a computer network system.
4 We _____ a new marketing manager.
5 We _____ our salaries to a good level.
6 We _____ our printing press problems.
7 We _____ in full colour.

16 Futures 2
future perfect and future perfect continuous

A Denise is 25 years old. She is studying for a research degree in agriculture. She is due to complete her course next year. She has just been to her elder brother's 35th birthday party and this has made her think about the next ten years of her own life. Choose which sentence ending, *a* or *b*, is correct.

1 In ten years I hope I'll
   a) be passing my final university exams.
   b) have passed my final university exams.

2 In ten years I hope I'll
   a) be earning a good salary.
   b) have earned a good salary.

3 In ten years I hope I'll
   a) be having two children.
   b) have had two children.

4 In ten years I hope I'll
   a) be writing my university thesis.
   b) have written my university thesis.

5 When Denise talks about an action *in progress* in ten years she uses
   a) future continuous – *I'll be doing*.
   b) future perfect – *I'll have done*.

6 When Denise talks about an action which will be *completed* in ten years she uses
   a) future continuous – *I'll be doing*.
   b) future perfect – *I'll have done*.

B Here are some more of Denise's thoughts about the next ten years. Complete her thoughts and write each one in the correct box. Use the future continuous or the future perfect.

live in a warmer climate   meet the 'right' person   work as an agriculturalist

pay back all the money   publish the results of my   live in a comfortable
my parents have lent me   research thesis   house

Actions in progress in ten years	Actions completed in ten years
I hope I _____	I hope I _____
I hope I _____	I hope I _____
I hope I _____	I hope I _____

C Denise is talking about her research work in agriculture. Complete what she says using one of the verbs from the box.

face   contribute   double   find   feed

By the year 2050, the Earth's population 1 _____ so there will be twice as many people. That means we 2 _____ twice as many people as today. I certainly hope that by then we 3 _____ much better ways of producing crops in order to do this; if not, there is no doubt in my mind that the world 4 _____ major problems. Of course, I hope my own research 5 _____ to any solutions that have been found.

Futures 3
mixed futures

17

You are in Britain travelling by train. Another passenger begins a conversation with you. Read the passenger's comments to you and then your thoughts about each comment. Use these thoughts and the verb on the right of the page to complete your replies to the passenger. You also need to use the most appropriate of the forms from the box.

> I'm ... ing
> I'm going to ...
> I'll ...
> I'll be ... ing
> Shall I ...?

The passenger's comments	Your thoughts	Your replies
Example: How far are you going?	You have a ticket to Cambridge.	*I'm getting off in Cambridge.* (get off)
1 Why Cambridge?	You have arranged to meet an old friend there.	Actually, _____ _____ (meet)
2 That's nice. Do you expect to stay long?	You have a ticket to leave on Sunday.	Not long, _____ _____ (leave)
3 Any ideas what to do there?	You have decided to visit the colleges.	Yes, _____ _____ (visit)
4 You really must see King's College Chapel.	You think this is a good idea, and you decide to go there too.	In that case, _____ _____ (go)
5 Hey, I could take you there if you're free at about three on Friday.	You have plans to work in the university library all Friday afternoon.	I'm afraid _____ _____ (work)
6 What a pity! Well, here's my phone number. Give me a ring if you like.	You wonder if 6.00 pm on Thursday is a good time to ring.	Let's see. _____ _____ (ring)
7 Did you know you can buy coffee on the train?	You didn't know so you decide to buy one.	In that case, I think _____ (buy)
8 Yes, it's quite good.	You want to offer the passenger a coffee too.	If it's good, _____ _____ (get)
9 Oh, no thanks. I have to get off soon.	You want to remind the passenger about your phone call on Thursday.	OK. I _____ _____ (ring)

© Will Forsyth, Sue Lavender 1995. Published by Heinemann English Language Teaching. This sheet may be photocopied and used within the class.

PHOTOCOPIABLE

18 If sentences 1

A Match each sentence with the correct picture, *a* or *b*.

1 If she didn't catch the train, she won't be here for dinner.

2 If she hadn't caught the train, she wouldn't have been here for dinner.

B Complete the dialogues using the words in *italics* in the correct form. Be careful; sometimes the *if* sentence describes something different from what happened, for example, '*If we hadn't invented paper* we wouldn't have had newspapers; in fact we did invent paper.' Sometimes the *if* sentence describes something that possibly happened, for example, '*If the Chinese didn't invent paper*, then who did?'

Example: **A:** Did Charles *get home late* last night?
B: I don't know. Why?
A: If he ___got home late___ he'll be tired when he gets up.

1 **A:** Did the British *go to America*?
  B: Yes, of course they did.
  A: If they _____ the American language would be Spanish, wouldn't it?

2 **A:** Did Helen *catch the 10 o'clock bus* or the 11 o'clock?
  B: I don't know. Why?
  A: If she _____ she'll be here soon.

3 **A:** Did the prisoner *have a gun*?
  B: No, he didn't. Why?
  A: If he _____ he might have killed someone.

4 **A:** My new shirt's too small.
  B: Did you *throw the receipt away*?
  A: No, I've still got it. Why?
  B: If you _____ you wouldn't have been able to take it back to the shop.

5 **A:** Richard took his exam yesterday.
  B: Did he *study hard*?
  A: I don't know. Why?
  B: If he _____ he'll probably have failed; he's not very good at Maths.

6 **A:** Did you *tell* Peter you saw me in town yesterday?
  B: No, I didn't.
  A: Thank goodness! If you _____ him, I'd have been in real trouble.

7 **A:** Did the director *come in* yesterday?
  B: No, she didn't. Why?
  A: If she _____ she'd want to know why I didn't.

8 **A:** Do you know if someone *has invented* a speaking watch?
  B: Yes, they have. Why?
  A: Because if they _____ one, I would.

9 **A:** Has the rain *stopped* yet?
  B: No. Why?
  A: If it _____ we could go out for a walk.

If sentences 2

A Put each of these *if* clauses into the correct box. You have to decide if they describe something which is/was possibly true, or something which is/was definitely not true.

possibly true	definitely not true
If the captain sent a radio signal	

Example: If the captain sent a radio signal before the ship sank …
1. If the captain had sent a radio signal before the ship sank …
2. If Les had been here now …
3. If Les is here now …
4. If Sarah said anything to your boss while you were away …
5. If Sarah had said anything to your boss while you were away …
6. If Ali had bought the tickets when the box office first opened …
7. If Ali bought the tickets when the box office first opened …
8. If I have any more food …
9. If I'd had any more food …

B Match each meaning on the left with the correct tense on the right.

1. If you mean that it is possibly true in the present/future …
2. If you mean that it was possibly true in the past …
3. If you mean that it is definitely not true in the past/present (and even future) …

a) you use *if* + the simple past (for example, *If he left early yesterday* …)
b) you use *if* + the past perfect (for example, *If he had left early* …)
c) you use *if* + the simple present (for example, *If he leaves early* …)

C Match each clause in part A with the correct ending below.

Example: If the captain had sent a radio signal before the ship sank,   a) we would have been rescued by now.

1. _____   b) they'll rescue us soon.
2. _____   a) we'll be able to ask him.
3. _____   b) we could have asked him.
4. _____   a) you'll be in trouble.
5. _____   b) you would have been in trouble.
6. _____   a) we'll have excellent seats.
7. _____   b) we would have got much better seats.
8. _____   a) I'd give it to you.
9. _____   b) I'll give it to you.

20 If sentences 3
mixed *if* sentences

You have just arrived to stay with a British friend at her house. Read the comments your friend makes to you and your thoughts about the comments. Then complete your replies using the word *if* in each reply and the two verbs in *italics* in the 'What you think' section.

What your friend says	What you think	What you say
Example: Why don't you stay longer? You'd be very welcome.	You would like to *stay*, but you don't have time.	If I _had time I'd stay longer._
1 Why didn't you ring me from the airport?	You didn't *have* any change so you didn't *ring*.	If I _____
2 Do make yourself at home here, won't you?	You are happy to *help* yourself to anything you *need*.	Don't worry. If I _____
3 You know, you really shouldn't have brought all these gifts!	You *wanted* to *bring* them.	I wouldn't _____
4 Why don't you come and meet some of my friends on Thursday?	You'd like to *come*, but you aren't sure if you *have* time.	I'll certainly _____
5 Now, can you remember all the things I've told you about Glasgow?	You aren't sure if you *remember*, but you can always *ring* her to ask.	Don't worry. _____
6 And why not visit Cornwall too while you're here?	You don't *have* enough money! But you would like to *go* there.	Well, I think I would _____
7 Is Stephanie meeting us next weekend?	You know she was hoping to *come*, but you don't know if she *got* a plane ticket.	I'm not sure. She'll _____
8 By the way, it was a good thing you managed to catch the bus this evening, wasn't it?	You are happy you *caught* it because you didn't want to *wait* until tomorrow morning for the next bus!	Yes, I'd still _____
9 You look tired! Why don't you have an early night?	You are *waiting* for a phone call so you can't *go* to bed.	I would _____

© Will Forsyth, Sue Lavender 1995. Published by Heinemann English Language Teaching. This sheet may be photocopied and used within the class.

Indirect questions 1   21

A You are staying with your friend, Liz. One morning Liz leaves you the following note.

```
Hi! I'm afraid I'm in a panic. The Dumals, (the French family I worked for last
year), have just rung to say that they're coming this weekend. If you have time
today, could you make the following phone calls for me?
    Bus station          time of first bus to Heathrow on Friday morning.
    Heathrow airport     arrival time for BA 272.
    Bargain Car Hire     cost of car hire for 2 days.
    Hill Guest House     double room available this weekend?
    Train station        cost of family day excursion ticket to London.
    Hong Hu Restaurant   open on Sunday evenings?
    Diana                come and meet them on Sunday?
Thanks a lot - you'll find all the numbers in my address book.   Liz
```

Now finish the questions you need to ask each person you ring.

Example: Bristol Bus Station   Could you tell me what time <u>the first bus to Heathrow on Friday morning is</u> ?

1 **Bristol Station**   Could you tell me how much _____?

2 **Hill Guest House**   I'd like to know _____.

3 **Bargain Car Hire**   A friend of mine would like to know how much _____.

4 **Heathrow**   I wonder if you can tell me what time _____?

5 **Hong Hu**   Could you tell me _____?

6 **Diana**   Liz wants to know whether _____?

B Here are some things the Dumals need to know. Complete the sentences by choosing a phrase or item from each box.

| if   what time   what   how long   whether   (how far)   how much | . ? |

Example: I'd like to know <u>how far</u> away the station is <u>.</u>
1 Could you tell us _____ the next bus arrives ____
2 Do you happen to know _____ or not the chemist is open late ____
3 Have you any idea _____ there's a market near here ____
4 We'd like to know _____ the flight takes ____
5 _____ do you think a ticket to Brighton costs ____
6 We were wondering _____ the name of this hotel was ____

22 Indirect questions 2

A In these two conversations David is talking on the phone to a shop-assistant and to a friend, Rita, about a new computer he wants to buy. Put the questions from the box into the correct conversation.

a) Do you happen to know which is the nearest bus stop for your shop?
b) Is that before or after tax?
c) And how much are they?
d) I don't suppose you remember how much your Roplex was?
e) Could you tell me if you have any Roplex XT1000Es in stock?

1 **David:** _____?
  Shop assistant: Yes, plenty.
  David: _____?
  Shop assistant: £985 excluding tax.
  David: _____?
  Shop assistant: Yes, Oxford Circus.

2 **David:** _____?
  Rita: About £1000, but it's difficult to remember.
  David: _____?
  Rita: Before, I'm afraid.

B Both of the conversations begin with indirect questions. Which of the following do you think are true about the use of indirect questions? Put a tick ✓ next to the ones which are true and a cross ✗ by any which are not.

1 You often use indirect questions to begin a conversation with someone you don't know well. ☐

2 Once you have begun a conversation with an indirect question it's normal to ask other questions in the same way. ☐

3 You often use indirect questions when you think your question is unusual or that someone might not know the answer. ☐

C David is talking to a passenger he has never met before at the bus stop. Change any questions *you think necessary* in the following conversation into indirect questions. Begin with 'Do you happen to know …' each time.

David: What time's the next bus due?

1 _____

Passenger: In about five minutes I think.
David: Great, not long, then. Does it go to Oxford Circus?

2 _____

Passenger: I hope so, that's where I'm going!
David: Oh, where's the Comsoft computer shop?

3 _____

Passenger: Never heard of it, I'm afraid.

Infinitive and gerund 1

23

What are these people saying? Complete their sentences using a verb from the box in the correct form.

| listen   watch   come   marry   feed   come   shout   go   tell   throw |

'Will you please be quiet; I'm trying _____ to the music.'

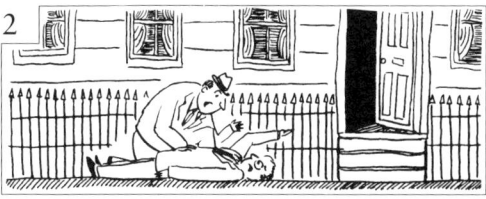

A: 'What happened?'
B: 'I don't know; I remember _____ out of the door, then nothing else.'

'I don't regret _____ him; but I wish I hadn't said I liked modern art.'

'If I'm working at home I often stop _____ the sun go down.'

'Why don't we try _____ it against the wall?'

'I regret _____ you that the next boat won't be until May.'

'Will you please stop _____ and calm down.'

'I must remember _____ the cat.'

'I'll never forget _____ here with you the first time just after we were married.'

'Oh no! I forgot _____ to the bank!'

© Will Forsyth, Sue Lavender 1995. Published by Heinemann English Language Teaching. This sheet may be photocopied and used within the class.

24 Infinitive and gerund 2

A Match each sentence with the correct picture, *a* or *b*.

1 She has stopped talking to him.

2 She has stopped to talk to him.

B Complete the second sentence each time. Use the words in *italics* in the first sentence in the infinitive with *to*, for example, *to leave* or the gerund, for example, *leaving*.

Example: I wish I hadn't *eaten* so much.
I regret ___eating___ so much; I've got a stomach ache.

1 I couldn't *light* the fire because the wood was wet.
I tried _____ the fire; but the wood was too wet.

2 I was cold so I *lit* the fire.
I was cold so I tried _____ the fire, but I still couldn't get warm.

3 I *teach* every day. I never normally walk out of a lesson, but yesterday I felt sick.
I stopped _____ and walked out of the class.

4 I was travelling through Arkansas when I was asked to stop and *teach* there for a while.
I was passing through Arkansas, but I stopped _____ there for a while.

5 I didn't *lock* my car at first, but then I saw a poster saying 'Beware of car thieves'.
I only remembered _____ my car when I saw a poster in the street.

6 I *went* to Greece as a child, but forgot all about it until saw the photographs.
I remembered _____ to Greece as a child when I saw the photographs.

7 We *went* to the beach. When I saw how far it was, I wished I hadn't gone.
I regretted _____ to the beach when I saw how far it was.

8 'I don't want to *tell* you this, but you must come with me to the station, sir.'
'I regret _____ you that you must accompany me to the station, sir.'

C Match the sentence halves on the left with the correct ending, *a* or *b*, on the right.

1	He stopped eating	a)	in a little restaurant outside Oxford.
2	He stopped to eat	b)	when he found an insect in his food.
3	I tried to tell him a joke	a)	but I couldn't remember it.
4	I tried telling him a joke	b)	but he still wouldn't laugh.
5	He stopped to smoke a cigarette	a)	but he still smokes cigars.
6	He stopped smoking cigarettes	b)	and then he went back to work.
7	Did you remember to go	a)	to Paris in 1979?
8	Do you remember going	b)	to the Post Office, or shall I go tomorrow?
9	I tried to push the car	a)	but I couldn't move it.
10	I tried pushing the car	b)	but the engine still wouldn't start.
11	I regret to tell you	a)	that you must leave this school forever.
12	I regret telling you	b)	my secret; you've told everyone.

© Will Forsyth, Sue Lavender 1995. Published by Heinemann English Language Teaching. This sheet may be photocopied and used within the class.

Infinitive and gerund 3   25

A Read what they did first and what they did second. Then decide which sentence they would say, *a* or *b*.

What they did first	What they did second	What they say
Example:		
He used to smoke a lot	but he stopped five years ago.	a) I stopped to smoke five years ago. b) I stopped smoking five years ago. *(circled)*
1 He was working but he stopped	and smoked a cigarette.	a) I stopped to smoke a cigarette. b) I stopped smoking a cigarette.
2 She remembered their appointment	so she met him at the restaurant.	a) I remembered to meet Jim. b) I remembered meeting Jim.
3 He met Yuka a long time ago	but he can still remember her.	a) I remember to meet Yuka. b) I remember meeting Yuka.
4 I told Lars and he told everyone	so now I regret it; everyone knows!	a) I regret to tell Lars my secret. b) I regret telling Lars my secret.
5 I don't want to tell you, but I must so	I'll tell you now, 'You must leave.'	a) I regret to tell you that you must leave. b) I regret telling you that you must leave.
6 I wanted to close the window,	and I tried, but I couldn't.	a) I tried to close the window. b) I tried closing the window.
7 The traffic was loud,	so I closed the window but I could still hear it.	a) I tried to close the window. b) I tried closing the window.

B Write each word or phrase in the correct box.

		Which action happened ...	
		FIRST	**SECOND**
Example: I remember seeing him. 1 I remembered to see him.	(remember/see)	*saw*	*remembered*
2 I stopped seeing him. 3 I stopped to see him.	(stop/see)		
4 I regret telling you. 5 I regret to tell you.	(regret/tell)		

C Match each sentence on the left with its ending, *a* or *b*, on the right.

1 I tried talking to him, but
2 I tried to talk to him, but

a) he wouldn't agree with anything I said.
b) they wouldn't let me in to see him.

3 'I tried talking to him' means
4 'I tried to talk to him' means

a) I couldn't talk to him.
b) I talked to him but it was no use.

26 Infinitive and gerund 4

A There are 14 verbs in the box. Seven are followed by an infinitive, for example, *agree to do* something, and seven by a gerund, for example, *admit doing* something. Put the verbs on the correct side of the scales. The scales must balance and have exactly 40 letters on each side.

> (agree) avoid   choose   deny   miss   plan   recall
> (admit) arrange consider decide manage practise refuse

A GREE
1 A
3 C
5 D
7 M
9 P
11 R

A DMIT
2 A
4 C
6 D
8 M
10 P
12 R

VERBS + INFINITIVE   VERBS + GERUND

B Here are two conversations which use some of the verbs from the scales above. Complete each conversation by using a verb from the box. You must decide whether to use a gerund or an infinitive.

> stay   meet   (see)   get   have

1 **A:** Sorry I missed _seeing_ you last week. I was feeling so ill that I decided 1 _____ in bed; that's why I didn't manage 2 _____ to the meeting.
  B: Well, never mind, we've arranged 3 _____ another meeting next week; we're planning 4 _____ at about two o'clock in the usual place.

> attack   give   steal   drop   see

2 **A:** The accused doesn't admit 5 _____ the money, and he certainly denies 6 _____ the cashier. The cashier is refusing 7 _____ evidence because she can't recall ever 8 _____ the accused before.
  B: In that case, I expect the police are considering 9 _____ the charges.

> go   speak   sit   visit

3 **A:** When I heard we could afford a holiday, I chose 10 _____ Italy. But then Roger said he wanted to avoid 11 _____ in the sun and he also wanted to practise 12 _____ German.
  B: So is that why you agreed 13 _____ to Germany instead?

PHOTOCOPIABLE

© Will Forsyth, Sue Lavender 1995. Published by Heinemann English Language Teaching. This sheet may be photocopied and used within the class.

Linking words 1
unless, as long as, in case, although

27

A Match the phrase from column A with a phrase from column B to make a complete sentence each time.

A
1 Take your camera in case
2 Take your camera unless
3 Take your camera as long as
4 Take your camera although

B
a) you don't mind carrying it.
b) mine doesn't work.
c) you haven't brought it.
d) you won't have much time for pictures.

B Your friend, Araceli, is going to visit London for the first time. Look at the questions she asks you about London. Use your thoughts with one of the expressions from the box to complete your answers to her questions.

| unless | as long as | in case | although |

Araceli's questions	Your thoughts	Your answers
Example: What do you think the weather will be like?	It's a good idea to take an umbrella as it might rain.	Bring an umbrella _in case it rains._
1 What's the best way to travel round the city?	The underground is fast and easy. It's only a problem if she wants to see the sights.	The underground is best _____
2 But isn't the underground very complicated?	You decide to give her a map because you think she might get lost.	Here's a map _____
3 What do you think about the Sunday markets?	You always enjoy them, but many people think they are too crowded.	Personally, I like them _____
4 And what about shopping in Oxford Street?	This is not a good idea, except if she wants to spend a lot of money.	I don't think it's a good idea _____
5 Do you think it's a good idea to see the Tower of London?	This is only a good idea if she can arrive early to avoid the crowds.	Yes, it's a good idea _____
6 What about that jazz club you mentioned?	It's possible to go. The problem is she will find it very noisy.	Yes, you could go, _____
7 Do you think I should try to get to Scotland?	This is a good idea, but only if she doesn't mind a long journey.	Sounds like a good idea _____
8 Is there anything else I should know?	It would be a good idea to bring extra money because she might want to buy a lot of presents.	Bring more money than you think you'll need _____

28 Linking words 2

although, in spite of, despite, because, however, due to, therefore

A Complete what the people in the pictures are saying by choosing one word from the box below each time.

> despite   because   spite
> due   however   although

1. Well, we got here _____ the weather!

2. _____ to bad weather conditions, all flights have been cancelled.

3. I can't come now _____ of the children.

4. _____ life was hard then, we were very happy.

5. He still gets around well in _____ of his leg.

6. ....well, he said he loved me. _____ I never saw him again.

B Here is some advice about holidays in Greenland. Match the beginning of each sentence with its correct ending.

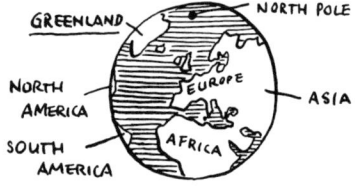

A
1. Because of
2. Although
3. If the weather is very bad,
4. Take some ice grips
5. It belongs to Denmark, therefore
6. Despite
7. In spite
8. You'll only be able to stay a short time

B
a) it's a good idea to book with a Danish company.
b) due to the high costs.
c) you'll probably have to stay in a hotel.
d) it's cold, transport usually still runs.
e) the extremely low temperatures you'll need protective clothing.
f) of the low temperatures, there's still a lot of sunshine.
g) in case you have the chance to go climbing.
h) the beauty of the fjords, it's still not a popular holiday resort.

© Will Forsyth, Sue Lavender 1995. Published by Heinemann English Language Teaching. This sheet may be photocopied and used within the class.

Linking words 3

although, in spite of, despite, because, however, due to, therefore

29

A Match each beginning on the left with its ending *a*, *b*, or *c* on the right.

A
1 Because
2 Because of
3 Due

B
a) the rain, we stayed at home.
b) it was raining, we stayed at home.
c) to the rain, we stayed at home.

4 He often felt the cold because
5 He often felt cold because of
6 He often felt cold due

a) having lived in India.
b) to having lived in India.
c) he had lived in India.

7 In spite
8 Despite
9 Although

a) the cost, we bought it.
b) of the cost, we bought it.
c) it was expensive, we bought it.

10 In spite
11 Despite
12 Although

a) she was ill, she came to the meeting.
b) of being ill, she came to the meeting.
c) being ill, she came to the meeting.

B Rewrite the following sentences using the word in brackets each time.

1 Because of the train strike, we took the car. (due)

2 Although I was hungry, I couldn't eat the snails. (despite)

3 In spite of the rough weather, the boat set sail. (although)

4 The economy collapsed, therefore the government resigned. (because)

5 They said the bridge wouldn't last; it is, however, still standing. (but)

6 Take my phone number; you might need it. (case)

C Here is part of a letter from Georges who has just visited Ireland. There are four mistakes in his letter; find them and correct them.

... I'm writing in case you will ever decide to go to Ireland. Despite of the bad weather, I had a wonderful time. Although I didn't have much money, it was still easy to find places to stay, and in spite of having been to Ireland twice before, I still found plenty of new things to see. Due to it an island, the weather can be quite changeable. It's a pity that because not having much free time I couldn't stay longer ...

30 Look, look like, look as if 1

Mrs Wallace has just moved into Lucas Street. Her new neighbours have different opinions of her. Look at the neighbours' thoughts and complete their answers. Use one of the three forms: *She looks/sounds ...; She looks/sounds like ...; She looks/sounds as if ...*

Mrs Wallace

A What does Mrs Wallace look like?

Mr Toms thinks ...   Mrs Porrit thinks ...   Mr Payne thinks ...

Example:
   She looks like   3 _____   6 _____
   a princess.   mean.   my old mother.
1 _____   4 _____   7 _____
   beautiful.   she'd murder you.   lonely.
2 _____   5 _____   8 _____
   she'll live forever.   an old witch.   she's had a hard life.

B What's she like to talk to?

Example:
   She sounds   3 _____   6 _____
   charming.   an old crow.   she wants someone to talk to.
1 Her voice _____   4 _____   7 _____
   _____ a silver bell.   she's hiding something.   a brave woman.
2 _____   5 _____   8 _____
   she grew up in a palace.   aggressive.   Polish.

PHOTOCOPIABLE

© Will Forsyth, Sue Lavender 1995. Published by Heinemann English Language Teaching. This sheet may be photocopied and used within the class.

Look, look like, look as if 2

31

A Each of these sentences describes one of the pictures. Write the name of each thing.

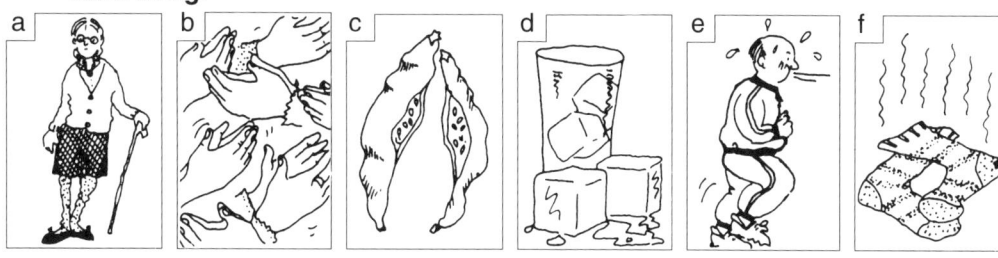

Example: It tastes like fire; it tastes as if it might burn your stomach away. c) *chilli pepper*
1 It feels hard and cold; it feels like a wet stone. _____
2 They smell horrible! They smell as if they have been used to keep cheese in for twenty years. _____
3 It sounds exciting. It sounds like waves on a beach. It sounds as though it could lift you and carry you away. _____
4 He looks as if he has been running; he looks hot and sweaty. _____
5 She looks old. She looks as though a breath of wind would blow her over. _____

B Put one of the following in each space <u>where necessary</u>: *like, as if* or *as though*.

1 Use _____ + adjective + noun, for example, *Monkeys look _____ old men.*

2 Use _____ + noun, for example, *A cat sometimes sounds _____ a baby crying.*

3 Use _____ + adjective, for example, *Cotton feels _____ soft.*

4 Use _____ or _____ + clause, for example, *It smells _____ something is burning.*

C Look at the pictures and complete each sentence with words from the two boxes.

| look   taste   smell   sound   feel | | —   like   as if/as though |

Example: It *feels* rough.

1 It _____ old fish.

2 It _____ sweet.

3 It _____ African music.

4 It _____ there's a party upstairs.

5 It _____ it's going to rain.

© Will Forsyth, Sue Lavender 1995. Published by Heinemann English Language Teaching. This sheet may be photocopied and used within the class.

PHOTOCOPIABLE

Modal verbs 1

Look at the pictures and complete what each person is saying using a verb from the box. Sometimes more than one verb is possible.

would   should   could   might

Example:

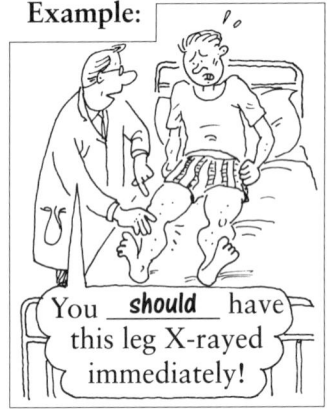

You _should_ have this leg X-rayed immediately!

1

_____ you pass me the sugar, please?

2

Be careful! You _____ fall!

3

When I was young I _____ play very well too.

4

If you went out now you _____ certainly get wet!

5

Yes, this _____ be the Leeds train. Oh look, it's written on the door.

6

Well, we _____ always take a taxi instead, what do you think?

7

Don't forget, you _____ win first prize!

8

When we were first engaged he _____ write to me every day. He never forgot.

Modal verbs 2

A Match the beginning of each sentence with the most appropriate ending, *a* or *b*.

1	You should wear a seat belt	a)	if you drive in Britain.
2	You would wear a seat belt	b)	if you drove in Britain.

3	If you applied for that job you would get it;	a)	but I don't really think you'd have very much chance.
4	If you applied for that job you might/could get it	b)	with your qualifications they'd be certain to take you.

5	It should be even warmer tomorrow;	a)	but I really hope not.
6	It might/could be even warmer tomorrow	b)	it said so on the forecast.

7	She could play the piano as a child	a)	but now she's forgotten how to.
8	She would play the piano as a child	b)	whenever guests came.

9	You could see a doctor about that	a)	I'm positive it needs medical attention.
10	You should see a doctor about that;	b)	but I don't think it's really necessary.

B Match the meanings below with the numbers of the sentences from part A. Note that some of the meanings match more than one sentence.

a) an ability someone had in the past _____
b) a habit someone had in the past _____
c) the certain outcome of an *if* clause __2__ and _____
d) the possible outcome of an *if* clause _____
e) strong advice for someone to do something __1__ and _____
f) a good outcome in the future based on strong evidence _____
g) the possibility that something will happen in the future _____
h) a suggestion for someone to do something _____

C Complete the sentence using a word from the box.

would should could might

Example: If you want someone to do something you ask if they __would__ or __could__ do it for you.

1 If you have strong evidence that something good will happen in the future you say it _____ happen.
2 If you think it's possible that something will happen in the future you say it _____ or _____ happen.
3 If you want to give someone strong advice you say they _____ do something.
4 If you want to make a suggestion you say someone _____ do something.
5 If you are talking about an ability in the past you say someone _____ do something.
6 If you are talking about a habit in the past you say someone _____ do something.
7 To talk about the certain outcome of an 'if' clause you use _____ .
8 To talk about the possible outcome of an 'if' clause you use _____ or _____ .

34 Modal verbs 3

A Jerry Lindsay is going to Guatemala for a year. His mother is worried about the trip. Write her questions using *will have to* or *will be able to* and a word or phrase from the box.

> come home   go camping   learn   (phone)   have   find a job   drive a car   write

Example: ___Will you be able to phone___ us?
Oh yes; it's possible to dial direct from there.

1 Mother: _____ there?
  Jerry: Not at first, I've saved enough money to last for a few months.
2 Mother: _____ Spanish while you're there?
  Jerry: Yes; not many people speak English there, but I want to anyway.
3 Mother: _____ in the countryside?
  Jerry: I certainly hope so; that's one of the reasons I want to go.
4 Mother: _____ to you?
  Jerry: Oh yes. I'll send you my address as soon as I can.
5 Mother: _____ there?
  Jerry: I think so; I've got an international driving licence.
6 Mother: _____ lots of injections?
  Jerry: I've already had them.
7 Mother: _____ if you really want to?
  Jerry: Yes, of course I will; I've always got my return ticket.

B A reporter is interviewing a student about politics. Complete the sentences with *can, must, be able to* or *have to* in the correct form and the verb in brackets. Sometimes you need to use *will*.

Reporter: ___Can I ask___ you a few questions about politics in your country?
Student: Yes, certainly.
Reporter: How old 1 _____ (be) to vote in your country?
Student: Eighteen; my age. I'm just eighteen.
Reporter: So you 2 _____ (vote) at the next election.
Student: That's right; for the first time.
Reporter: Do you know who you're going to vote for?
Student: I'm not sure. If the national party wins we 3 _____ (start) doing national service and they'll cut spending on education so a lot of people 4 _____ (not go) to university, but at the same time we 5 _____ (not pay) so much tax.
Reporter: Are most people very interested in politics in your country?
Student: Oh yes, a lot of people think we 6 _____ (keep) the national party out at all costs and get the social party in.
Reporter: Do you think they 7 _____ (do) that?
Student: I don't know. We 8 _____ (see).

Modal verbs 4

A Put each phrase from the box into the correct picture.

won't be able to   can't

1 You _____ drive ever again!

2 You _____ drive: you're much too young.

B In the following dialogues put a tick in the box if the sentences are possible. Sometimes only one sentence is possible, but sometimes both *a* and *b* are possible.

Example:
We're going to Ulaan Baatar next month;
    a) can we telephone direct from there? ✓
    b) will we be able to telephone direct from there? ✓

1 They're putting in an international phone line next month;
    a) can we telephone direct then?
    b) will we be able to telephone direct then?

2 My legs are badly broken, aren't they, doctor?
    a) Yes, but you can walk again in eight months or so.
    b) Yes, you'll be able to walk again in eight months or so.

3 I feel much better now, doctor.
    a) Yes, you can leave at the end of the week.
    b) Yes, you'll be able to leave at the end of the week.

4 We don't have to study foreign languages at the moment, but Mrs Vine becomes head teacher next year
    a) and then we have to study French or German.
    b) and then we'll have to study French or German.

5 When you go to senior school
    a) you have to study French or German.
    b) you'll have to study French or German.

C Match each sentence beginning with its correct ending.

1 You use *can* to say that   a) it is not yet possible (but it will be).

2 You use *will be able to* to say that   b) it is possible now (to do it now or in the future).

3 You use *must* or *have to* to say that   c) it is necessary now (to do it now or in the future).

4 You use *will have to* to say that   d) it is not necessary yet (but it will be).

36 Modal verbs 5
would/should/could have done referring to the past

A Alan went sailing and got lost in a storm. He was rescued by a ship. When the captain heard Alan's story, he was not very sympathetic. Complete the captain's sentences using the words in brackets with *should*, *would* or *could/might* (in this situation *could* and *might* mean the same thing) in the correct form.

Don't your realise you ____could have drifted____ (drift) for days? You 1 _____ (even die) if we hadn't seen you. You 2 _____ (listen) to the weather forecast before you left and you 3 _____ (check) your petrol supply. You 4 _____ (not go) sailing again until you learn to do it properly. You were lucky we found you; we 5 _____ (easily miss) you out in the open sea and then you 6 _____ (be) in real trouble. If you went to classes you 7 _____ (know) what to do and you 8 _____ (learn) to be a real sailor, though I'm not sure of that. You 9 _____ _____ (take) some waterproof clothes and a life jacket when you set out, and you 10 _____ (tell) someone where you were going. In fact, you 11 _____ (go out) at all as the weather's been so changeable recently. If you had died it 12 _____ (be) all your own fault, and you're not a child either; you 13 _____ (know) better. You 14 _____ (still catch) influenza, so keep warm.

B Use a modal from the box and the underlined verb to complete what each speaker says.

| should   could   would   might/could |

1 I'm sorry I didn't <u>do</u> it, but if there'd been time I certainly _____.
2 I <u>bought</u> some shoes which didn't fit me; I _____.
3 He was miles away when it was <u>stolen</u> so he _____.
4 Lola <u>took</u> the train. If the plane hadn't been so expensive, she _____.
5 I still haven't <u>rung</u> her although I know I _____.

Modal verbs 6

would/should/could have done referring to the present and future

A Complete the sentences with a verb from the box. If two answers are possible, for example, *I would leave* or *I would have left*, give both.

> finish   stop   go   fall   look   (reach)   lend   find   grow

1. We get into port tomorrow; we should **have reached** port today but we lost time in the storm.

2. If I'd ordered the tickets earlier I could _____ on the China tour next summer, but I can't now.

3. I would _____ it to you this afternoon but, as you can see, it's broken.

4. Some scientists believe we might _____ a cure for cancer by the end of this decade.

5. I would _____ the report before the end of this week only my computer broke.

6. All the leaves should _____ by the beginning of December.

7. It would _____ to thirty metres but for the storm.

8. It would _____ nice in the garden.

9. With motorbikes we could _____ them before the bridge.

B Harry is having some trouble with the builders. Complete the conversation using the verbs in brackets and one of these modals: *might, could, should* or *would*. If two answers are possible, give both.

Harry: I thought you said the house **would be finished** (finish) before next year.
Builder: Yes, well, it 1 _____ (be) for sure but for the rain. We 2 _____ (finish) building the house by winter if we'd been able to dig the foundations earlier and we 3 _____ (dig) them last week if we wanted to keep to the plan.
Harry: But we do want to keep to the plan.
Builder: Yes, we 4 _____ (certainly/finish) the foundations earlier, but with all the flooding the house 5 _____ (fall) down too.
Harry: I see. So what's the new timetable?
Builder: If all goes well we 6 _____ (finish) the interior by spring, and if so, you 7 _____ (move) in before the summer.

38 Modal verbs 7

A Match each sentence on the left with one on the right.

1 Do you know what the next stop is? a) It could/might/should have been Leeds.
2 Do you know what the last stop was? b) It could/might/should be Leeds.

3 How many of these tablets do I take? a) You should only have taken one.
4 Those tablets made me feel sick. b) You should only take one.

5 Why not come to the party tomorrow? a) I'm sure you would enjoy it.
6 Why didn't you come to the party yesterday? b) I'm sure you would have enjoyed it.

7 He might/should/would stay a) always refers to the present/future.
8 He might/should/would have stayed b) often refers to the past.

B Match the beginning of each sentence on the left with its ending, *a* or *b*, on the right.

1 It's a shame Sarah's gone abroad; a) I'm sure she'd enjoy this party.
2 Let's give Sarah a ring and ask her to come b) I'm sure she'd have enjoyed this party.

3 If they haven't sold all the tickets yet a) I might/could leave tomorrow.
4 I wish they hadn't sold all the tickets; b) I might/could have left tomorrow.

5 She would/could/might stay a) refers to a future which is still possible.
6 She would/could/might have stayed b) often refers to a present/future which is no longer possible.

C Put a tick ✓ against the endings which are possible. Sometimes both *a* and *b* are possible, sometimes only one of them is.

1 Why not wait here until 7.00?   a) He might/could/should phone by then.
   b) He might/could/should have phoned by then.
2 Why not get here at 7.00?
   a) He might/could/should phone any time after then.
   b) He might/could/should have phoned any time after then.
3 To get the diploma you
   a) should attend 1000 hours by the end of the course.
   b) should have attended 1000 hours by the end of the course.
4 We'll let him take the exam again at the end of the week;
   a) he might/could understand calculus by then.
   b) he might/could have understood calculus by then.
5 Paris is such a beautiful city;
   a) everybody should go there at least once in their life.
   b) everybody should have been there at least once in their life.
6 It might/could/should/would have happened
   a) can refer to the past, present or future.
   b) can only refer to the present/future.
7 It might/should/would happen   a) can refer to the past, present or future.
   b) can only refer to the present/future.

© Will Forsyth, Sue Lavender 1995. Published by Heinemann English Language Teaching. This sheet may be photocopied and used within the class.

Modal verbs 8

must, might, could and *can't* for deduction

A Here are three photos. Decide which comment refers to which picture and write the letter of the comment in the box under the picture.

1 2 *Example* 3

i) **Example:** It must be cold.
    a) It might be cold.
    b) It can't be cold.

ii) c) People can't be working today.
    d) People must be working today.
    e) People might be working today.

iii) f) It might have been snowing.
    g) It can't have been snowing.
    h) It must have been snowing.

iv) i) The picture could have been taken in Britain.
    j) The picture couldn't have been taken in Britain.
    k) The picture must have been taken in Britain.

B Here are some explanations of the comments above. Write the letter of each comment before the appropriate explanation. Note that the numbers, (i to iv), refer to the comments under the same number in part A.

i) **Example:** __Example__ because everyone is wearing thick coats.
   1 _____ because everyone is wearing summer clothes.
   2 _____ because the wind is blowing.

ii) 3 _____ because all the shops and offices are open.
   4 _____ because there is a lot of traffic in the street.
   5 _____ because all the shops and offices are closed.

iii) 6 _____ because the ground looks white.
    7 _____ because it looks quite cold.
    8 _____ because the sun is shining and the flowers are blooming.

iv) 9 _____ because people are driving on the right.
   10 _____ because the signs are written in English.
   11 _____ because there is a British flag flying.

Modal verbs 9

must, *might*, *could* and *can't* for deduction

A Read the information on the left and then use the verbs in the boxes to complete the comments.

| might   won't   will   could |

1 In winter, it's always cold in Mongolia. It's sometimes sunny and it sometimes snows. It's never foggy.

So when we get to Mongolia next winter it (a) _____ be sunny, it (b) _____ be foggy, but it (c) _____ be cold and it (d) _____ be snowing.

| could   must   can't   might |

2 Colin is tall with a moustache. Paul is tall and has grey hair. Deb is short and has grey hair.

I can see someone coming: it's someone with grey hair, it (a) _____ be Deb, or it (b) _____ be Paul, but it certainly (c) _____ be Colin. Ah yes, I can see better now; it's a man and he's quite tall so it (d) _____ be Paul.

| must have   might have   could have   can't have |

3 **A:** Have you ever seen 'Purple Turtles'? It's a great film!

B: No, I've never heard of it so I'm sure I (a) _____ seen it.
C: Well, it sounds a bit familiar; I think I (b) _____ seen it.
D: I'm not sure; I can never remember films, but I (c) _____ seen it.
C: Oh yes, I remember it! I (d) _____ seen it years ago!

| might have   can't have   could have   must have |

4 Jasper has arrived in Budapest and has just realised that he has lost his passport.

I (a) _____ had it when I got off the plane because I showed it at immigration control. Then, I (b) _____ left it at immigration control because I showed it later at customs. After that I (c) _____ put it back in my bag, or I (d) _____ put it in my pocket, but I can't remember which.

B Complete the sentences using the verbs in the box in the correct form.

| will   can   could   must   might |

Example: When you are sure about something in the future you say it __will__ or __won't__ happen.

1 When you think it possible that something will happen in the future you say it _____ or _____ happen.
2 When you are sure that something is true you say it _____ be true.
3 When you are sure that something isn't true you say it _____ or _____ be true.
4 When you think it possible that something is true you say it _____ or _____ be true.
5 When you are sure that something has happened in the past you say it _____ happened.
6 When you are sure that something didn't happen in the past you say it _____ or _____ happened.
7 When you think it possible that something happened in the past you say it _____ or _____ happened.

Modal verbs 10

could, be able to and *manage to*

41

A Yesterday, Steven Johnson, aged 52, rescued a boat with two children in it. These pictures show you what happened.

Here is part of an interview between Steven and a reporter about the rescue. Use the verbs given to complete Steven's replies. Use one of the following in every answer:

| managed, for example, *I managed to find* | could, for example, *I could find* |
| just the verb, for example, *I found* | couldn't, for example, *I couldn't find* |

Reporter

Steven, could you tell us what happened?

Did you know there were children in it?

Why didn't you tell the life guard?

So what did you do?

Were you frightened?

Was the sea rough?

What happened then?

Wasn't the boat very heavy?

Steven

Yes, I was walking along by the harbour when I ___saw___ (see) the boat about 400 metres away.

Well, 1 _____ (hear) crying, which I thought was coming from the boat.

I tried to, but I 2 _____ (phone) because the telephone wasn't working.

I 3 _____ (decide) to swim out and get it myself.

I suppose I was, really, but when I was young I 4 _____ (swim) six miles without much trouble, so I thought I'd try it again.

Yes, very, and I nearly went under a couple of times, but finally I 5 _____ (swim) to the boat and then I just 6 _____ (climb) on board without any trouble.

There was an engine on board, but I 7 _____ (start) it, so I 8 _____ (find) some oars and 9 _____ (begin) rowing.

Yes, it was, and I'm not young any more, but slowly I 10 _____ (row) the boat back into harbour.

B Choose the most appropriate form, *a* or *b*, for each sentence.

1 Nigel   a) couldn't   win the competition today, but he
          b) didn't manage to   did come second.

2 The tourists   a) could   complete the tour even though the
                b) managed to   coach broke down.

3 Astrid   a) could   get in last night even though she lost
         b) was able to   her key.

4 The pilot   a) couldn't   fly at night because he had no lights.
            b) didn't manage to

© Will Forsyth, Sue Lavender 1995. Published by Heinemann English Language Teaching. This sheet may be photocopied and used within the class.

42 Modal verbs 11
could, *be able to* and *manage to*

A Match the sentences on the left with the explanations on the right. To do so, decide if the sentence is describing someone's general past ability to do something, or a single action in the past when someone succeeded in doing something.

1 He could sing beautifully as a child.
2 He was feeling sick but he managed to sing the song right to the end.

a) a single action
b) a general ability

3 Apparently, she was able to walk before she was one year old.
4 She had broken a leg, but she was still able to walk to a house for help.

a) a single action
b) a general ability

5 The horse escaped last night and we couldn't catch it.
6 I couldn't swim until I was about 20 years old.

a) a single action
b) a general ability

7 I didn't stop her because I simply wasn't able to.
8 I've never been able to dance.

a) a single action
b) a general ability

B Read the three explanations and the examples. One of them is not possible. Which one?

1 *managed* = a successful action
"In yesterday's cycle race she managed to finish first and Mr Smith came second."

2 *could* = an ability someone had
"She could cycle 60 miles a day when she was 50."

3 *could* = a successful action
"In yesterday's cycle race she could finish first and Mr Smith came second."

C Correct *could/manage to* in the following sentences only if necessary.

1 She managed to cycle up the hill on her eightieth birthday.
2 Last Friday she could cycle up the hill in under five minutes for the first time.
3 She managed to cycle up the hill every day until the day she died.
4 She could cycle up the hill until the day she died.
5 She could go shopping easily when she had her bicycle.
6 Everyone was surprised when she lost the race because they knew that she managed to cycle faster than anyone else in the village.

Passives 1

43

Look at the picture and answer the question using the verb given. The answer always begins *I'm afraid it ...* . Be careful: the tense in your answer should be the same as that in the question.

1. What's happened to the train?
I'm afraid it's _been cancelled._ (cancel)

2. What's happened to your car?
I'm afraid it's _____ (steal)

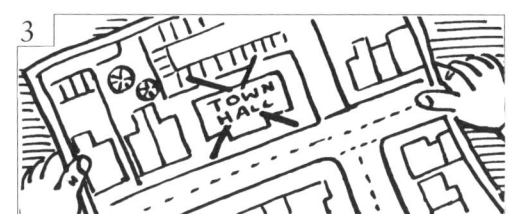

3. What's going to happen to the old town hall? I'm afraid it's _____ _____ (demolish)

4. What's happened to our house?
I'm afraid it _____ (burgle)

5. What do you think will happen to the airport if the holiday trade increases?
I'm afraid it _____ (enlarge)

6. What's happening to the traffic during the procession?
I'm afraid it _____ (divert)

7. What's happened to the sign?
I'm afraid it _____
(knock down)

8. What happens to the waste paper?
I'm afraid it _____
(throw away)

9. What's happened to our hotel?
I'm afraid it _____ yet.
(build)

10. What's happening to my wife?
I'm afraid she _____
(interview)

© Will Forsyth, Sue Lavender 1995. Published by Heinemann English Language Teaching. This sheet may be photocopied and used within the class.

PHOTOCOPIABLE

44 Passives 2

A   Match each sentence with the correct picture, *a* or *b*.

1 He's stopped.
2 He's been stopped.

3 The party has ended.
4 The party has been ended.

5 The car's moving.
6 The car's being moved.

7 Don't worry it's going to change.
8 Don't worry it's going to be changed.

B   Match the beginning of each sentence with the most appropriate ending, *a* or *b*.

1 I gave
2 I was given

a) everybody my address.
b) everybody's address.

3 This tiger killed
4 This tiger was killed

a) by two hunters.
b) two hunters.

5 Pam has her own car because
6 Pam has her own chauffeur because

a) she likes being driven.
b) she likes driving.

7 Ian's a music teacher now;
8 Ian's a music student now;

a) he's being taught the piano.
b) he's teaching the piano.

9 At the reunion
10 At the funeral

a) he remembered all his old friends.
b) he was remembered by all his old friends.

© Will Forsyth, Sue Lavender 1995. Published by Heinemann English Language Teaching. This sheet may be photocopied and used within the class.

Passives 3

45

A Decide which phrase, *a* or *b*, best completes each excerpt.

1 COLLEGE GUIDE

The college was founded early in the eighteenth century, and some of the present buildings date from that time.
a) **The buildings which today form the main quadrangle were added**
b) **They added the buildings which today form the main quadrangle**
early this century. The remaining out-buildings were completed between the wars when the college took on much of the appearance it has today.

2 QUEEN VISITS BRIDLINGTON

The Queen was dressed in a white suit with blue trim. She was wearing a white scarf and carried other white accessories.
a) **Her suit was specially designed for the occasion by Gocci.**
b) **Gocci specially designed her suit for the occasion.**
She was accompanied by her husband, the Duke, who also wore blue.

3 THE TELEPHONE: A MODERN CONVENIENCE

The telephone is now very much a part of modern life.
a) **Alexander Graham Bell first invented it and**
b) **First invented by Alexander Graham Bell,**
there is now at least one telephone in most British households. In fact, recent statistics show …

B Here are some excerpts from newspaper articles. There is a sentence, or part of a sentence, missing from each article. Use the pictures to decide what the missing words should be. Include the verb given. Be careful; you need to decide if the missing phrase should be active or passive!

1 BANK ROBBERY

Early yesterday morning robbers broke into Smith's bank. _____ (steal) and then drove away in a stolen vehicle.

2 CAR FACTORY TO CLOSE

Residents of Malham were yesterday shocked at the news that their local car paint plant is to close. Cars are at present assembled in nearby Dewby and then brought to Malham where _____ (paint). A local spokesman said the news could well mean the loss of over 100 jobs.

3 CENTENARIAN ADMITTED TO HOSPITAL

In the early hours of this morning, Mrs Anna Kay of 21 Louth Drive was rushed into the Ace hospital. Relatives said she had earlier complained of difficulty in breathing. On admission _____ (examine) and it was decided that an early operation was essential. It is hoped she can be home in time for her 101st birthday next week.

46 Passives 4

NEW HELEN O'NEILL FILM SOON TO BE RELEASED

1 Fans will be pleased to hear Helen O'Neill has made a new film entitled *Dusty Moonlight*. 2 It is the story of a young girl who moves from Ireland to Spain. 3 They shot the film entirely on location in Ireland and Spain. 4 Luca Lopez directed it and Pablo Mendes produced it. 5 People say Ms O'Neill's costumes are outstanding. 6 Gocci specially designed her dresses. 7 They have already nominated the film for several awards. 8 It is due to open in Edinburgh this summer.

A In the above press report some of the sentences seem out of place. This is because the main subjects of the report are Helen O'Neill and her new film and some sentences have been given a different subject:

Example: 3 They shot the film entirely on location in Ireland and Spain.

This sounds out of place because we do not know who 'they' are. It is more natural to relate other information to the main subject:

Example: 3 The film was shot entirely on location in Ireland and Spain.

Look at the sentences in the report again and write what you think the subject of each sentence should be. Some of them have already been done for you.

1 Helen O'Neill
2 It (the film)
3 The film
4 _____
5 _____
6 _____
7 _____
8 _____

B Use the new subjects from part A to complete the re-writing of the press report. Look at those sentences which have already been completed first. Notice that you do not need to change all the sentences.

1 Helen O'Neill has made a new film entitled Dusty Moonlight.
2 It is the story of a young girl who moves from Ireland to Spain.
3 The film was shot entirely on location in Ireland and Spain.
4 _____
5 _____
6 _____
7 _____
8 _____

C Here is a short passage about Marco Polo's introduction of pasta to Italy. Use the words in the box below to complete the passage. Note that you need to use some of the words more than once.

| Marco Polo | it | he | discovery | Italy | China | pasta |

Many people are surprised to learn that 1 _____ was first introduced into 2 _____ by 3 _____ who discovered 4 _____ during his travels in 5 _____ . 6 _____ probably had little idea how significant his 7 _____ would turn out to be. After its introduction, 8 _____ was quickly adopted as a national dish throughout 9 _____ . Today, 10 _____ is produced commercially all over the country and 11 _____ even exports several varieties to 12 _____ !

Past and present

A Complete each person's question using *you* and the verb given.

1. When _____ the change? (notice)

2. Why _____ your dog? (shave)

3. How long _____ ? (wait)

4. How many times _____ this before? (do)

5. How fast _____ at the time of the accident? (drive)

6. How many people _____ every day? (meet)

B Complete the story using the verbs given.

It was while I 1 _____ (live) in New Mexico that I first 2 _____ (realise) that I 3 _____ (be) on this earth before. One day at dawn I 4 _____ (climb) over the Aztec ruins, when, in the sun's first light, I suddenly 5 _____ (see) pictures that 6 _____ (draw) by Aztec priests almost one thousand years before. Staring at me from the stone 7 _____ (be) a face I 8 _____ (recognise) as my own. It 9 _____ (be) then that the dreams 10 _____ (begin), which 11 _____ (haunt) me ever since, of the days when I 12 _____ (sacrifice) men's immortal souls to the sun.

48 Pasts 1
past and past perfect, simple and continuous

Complete the story using the verbs below each picture.

---

be   drive   can

It __was__ early morning. I
1 _____ all night to get to
Sheila before she 2 _____
leave for South America.

---

get   check   not return   go

I 3 _____ to the hotel at
6 a.m. I 4 _____ that Sheila
5 _____ from the nightclub
and 6 _____ up to her room.

**go   hear   wonder   follow
wait   be   leave**

As I 7 _____ upstairs, I 8 _____
someone else going to the desk.
I 9 _____ if someone 10 _____ me to
the hotel. I 11 _____ to see who it
12 _____, but after a few words with
the clerk, they just 13 _____ again.

---

be   go   slip   not be   have

When I 14 _____ sure they
15 _____ , I 16 _____ into
Sheila's room. As she 17 _____
there, I 18 _____ plenty of time
to prepare.

---

come   wait

When Sheila 19 _____ in, I
20 _____ for her.

---

not look   see   tell

She 21 _____ surprised when
she 22 _____ me. Someone
23 _____ her to expect me.

---

give   drink   feel   fall

She 24 _____ me a drink. I
25 _____ it. I 26 _____
_____ a pain in my stomach and
27 _____ on the floor.

---

kill   say   not be   confess   hide

'Now you'll never tell anyone that I
28 _____ Floosie Moore,'
she 29 _____ . But it
30 _____ important; she
31 _____ and I
32 _____ microphones all
over the room.

Pasts 2

A Choose the correct ending for each of the following sentences, *a* or *b*.

1 I pretended I was asleep
2 I pretended I'd been asleep
   a) so I said 'What time is it?' and yawned.
   b) so I didn't move a muscle.

3 John repaired it because he did it
4 John repaired it because he'd done it
   a) all the time in his job.
   b) before.

5 When the manager arrived, they were robbing the bank
6 When the manager arrived they had robbed the bank
   a) so she wasn't able to see the robbers herself.
   b) so she was able to see the robbers herself.

7 She said it was raining
8 She said it had been raining
   a) so we would need an umbrella.
   b) but that now it was clear.

9 The past perfect is used
10 The past simple or continuous is used
   a) for an action completed before other past actions began.
   b) either for a single action or for actions that happened at about the same time.

B Decide which is the correct phrase to complete the sentence.

1 They felt exhausted that morning because *they drove/they had been driving* all night.
2 The village *was deserted/had been deserted* for years when we first visited it.
3 She understood the company's problems because she *worked/had worked* there since it started.
4 He *died/had died* at the moment he hit the ground.

C These pairs of sentences are identical except that the first sentence contains the past simple while the second contains the past perfect. Write *different* if the past perfect changes the meaning of the previous sentence and *same* if it does not.

Example: I knew he didn't lie./I knew he hadn't lied. ____different____

1 They only arrived after I left./They only arrived after I had left. _____
2 She visited a woman who worked for the CIA./She visited a woman who had worked for the CIA. _____
3 He asked me if I ever sold antiques./He asked me if I had ever sold antiques. _____
4 They wouldn't let us in until we showed them our identity cards./They wouldn't let us in until we had shown them our identity cards. _____

D Match each beginning on the left with its correct ending on the right.

1 The past perfect is not usually necessary to indicate a move backwards in time …
2 The past perfect is usually necessary to show a move back in time …

a) … in indirect speech and if there is no conjunction.
b) … if conjunctions such as *after, before* and *until* already make the move clear.

50 Pasts 3

Frances is 80 years old. She is looking at some objects she has kept for many years and is telling a friend the story of why she never got married.

> I was in love with and engaged to a soldier. His name was Tom, but he was killed during the war …

Complete what Frances says about the objects using the verbs given.

Example:

wear   get married

Here's the dress I _was going to wear_ when we _got married_ .

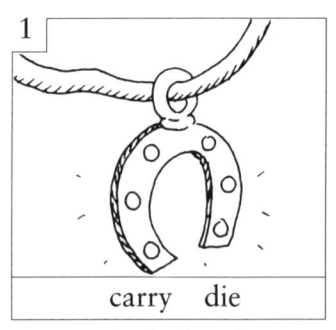

1

carry   die

Here's the lucky charm he _____ when he _____ .

2

give   promise

Here's the ring he _____ me when I _____ to marry him.

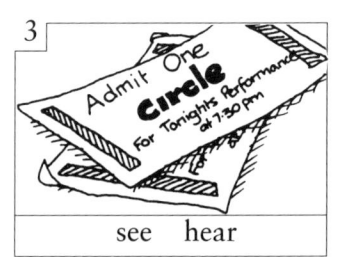

3

see   hear

Here are the unused tickets for a play we _____ _____ the night I first _____ he was dead.

4

wear   see

Here's the dress I _____ _____ the first time I _____ him.

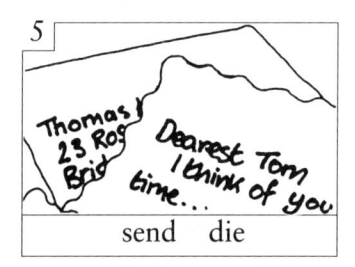

5

send   die

Here's the letter, still unfinished, that I _____ _____ him the night he _____ .

6

tell   write

Here's a poem he _____ me he _____ specially for me.

7

take   meet

Here's the photo he _____ the first time I _____ his family.

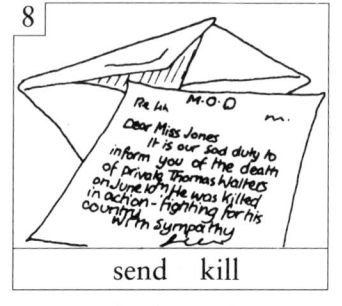

8

send   kill

Here's the letter they _____ _____ to tell me that he _____ .

Pasts 4

A Here are some photographs Sherry took on her holiday. They are of two friends, Alex and Karen. Complete what she says about each photograph using the verb given.

Example:
When I took this one, _Alex had (just) fallen into the river._ (fall)

1 When I took this one, Alex and Karen _____ (climb)
2 When I took this one, Karen _____ (get up)
3 When I took this one, Alex and Karen _____ (eat)
4 When I took this one, Alex _____ (have)
5 When I took this one, the film _____ (finish)

B Match the meaning of the verb with each picture with the explanations below and write the number of each picture in the correct place.

a) an action completed before the photograph _Example_ _____ _____
b) an action already in progress at the time of the photograph _____ _____
c) an action only at the same time as the photograph _____ _____
d) an action to start after the photograph _____ _____

52 Prepositions 1

A You are interviewing Peter Schanks, world tennis champion. Fill in the missing prepositions and then put the answers in the puzzle to find the hidden word.

Example: When did you arrive __in__ this country?
1. And how long are you planning to stay here ____ ?
2. Are you looking forward ____ the championship?
3. Are you afraid ____ losing your title this year, Peter?
4. What do you feel your success has been due ____ ?
5. Do you believe ____ training every day?
6. How many of this year's competitions will you be involved ____ ?
7. And which competition are you most interested ____ winning?
8. What type of tennis do you think you're best ____ ?
9. Who did you pick up most of your techniques ____ ?
10. Finally, Peter, are you fond ____ other types of sport?

B Match each expression with the correct preposition to find out what sorts of people Alice likes and dislikes.

Expressions	
take advantage ____ other people.	never criticise you ____ your back.
can't take pleasure ____ simple things.	need to have a reason ____ everything
disagree ____ me sometimes, but not always.	are enthusiastic ____ what they are doing.
I can depend ____ .	frequently get ____ control.
remember people ____ name.	laugh ____ other people's misfortunes.

I like people who ...   I don't like people who ...

Example: about: _are enthusiastic_   5 of: _____
about what they are doing.

1 on: _____   6 for: _____

2 by: _____   7 out of: _____

3 behind: _____   8 in: _____

4 with: _____   9 at: _____

Prepositions 2

A You want to use the objects in the pictures but you don't know their names in English. How do you explain what you want each time? Use a preposition from the box to complete each of your descriptions.

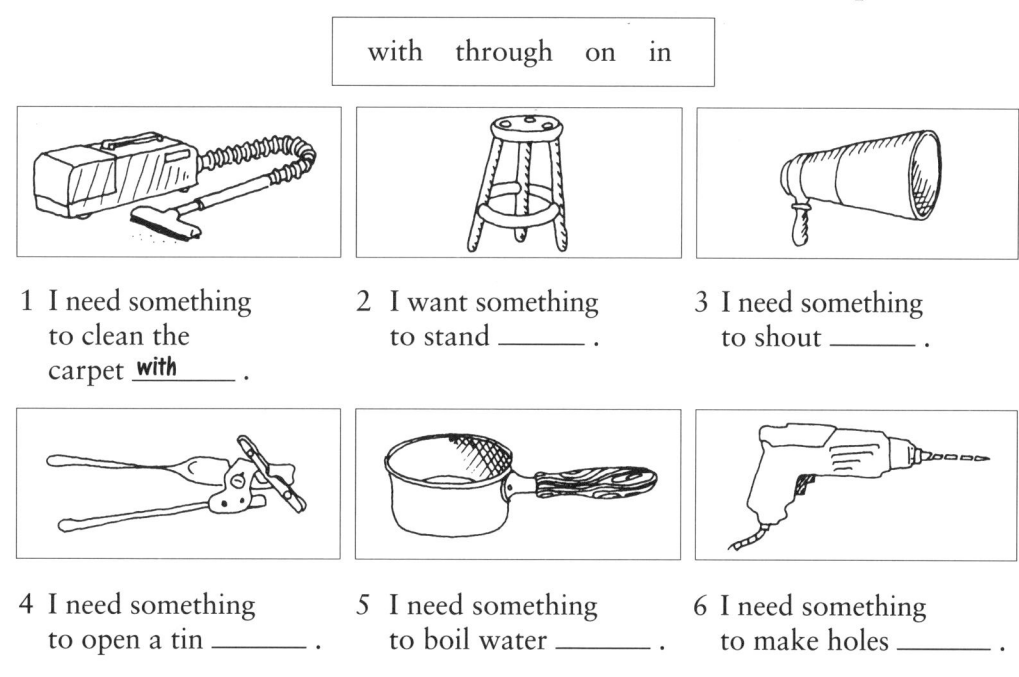

with   through   on   in

1 I need something to clean the carpet **with** ____ .

2 I want something to stand _____ .

3 I need something to shout _____ .

4 I need something to open a tin _____ .

5 I need something to boil water _____ .

6 I need something to make holes _____ .

B Complete the answers to the questions. The pictures will help you. Include a preposition from the box.

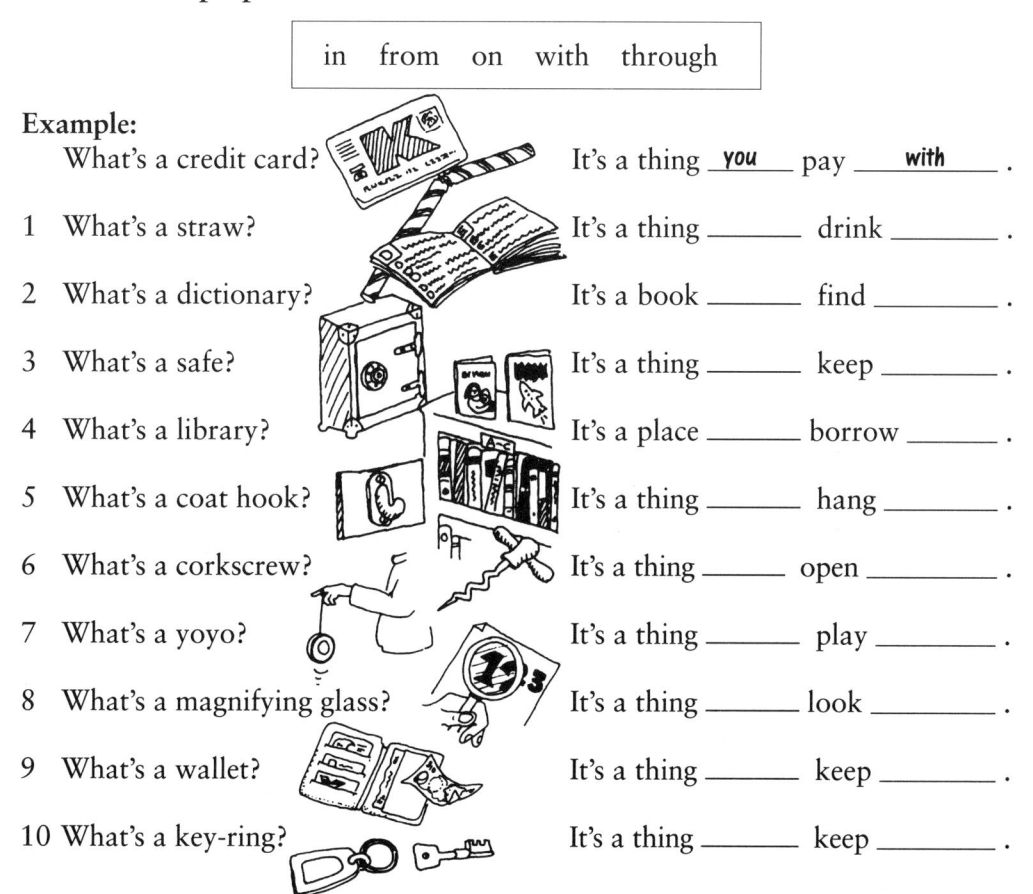

in   from   on   with   through

Example:
What's a credit card?   It's a thing **you** pay **with** ____ .

1 What's a straw?   It's a thing ____ drink ____ .

2 What's a dictionary?   It's a book ____ find ____ .

3 What's a safe?   It's a thing ____ keep ____ .

4 What's a library?   It's a place ____ borrow ____ .

5 What's a coat hook?   It's a thing ____ hang ____ .

6 What's a corkscrew?   It's a thing ____ open ____ .

7 What's a yoyo?   It's a thing ____ play ____ .

8 What's a magnifying glass?   It's a thing ____ look ____ .

9 What's a wallet?   It's a thing ____ keep ____ .

10 What's a key-ring?   It's a thing ____ keep ____ .

© Will Forsyth, Sue Lavender 1995. Published by Heinemann English Language Teaching. This sheet may be photocopied and used within the class.

PHOTOCOPIABLE

54 Present perfect and past simple 1

A Match each sentence with the correct picture, *a* or *b*.

1. We've had a really good day.
2. We had a really good day.
3. It's grown to a huge size.
4. It grew to a huge size.

B Match the beginning of each sentence with its correct ending, *a* or *b*.

1. I've lost my key
2. I lost my key
   - a) so I couldn't get in.
   - b) so I can't get in.

3. I changed my mind
4. I've changed my mind
   - a) so I didn't go.
   - b) so I'm not going.

5. I lived here for five years;
6. I've lived here for five years;
   - a) and I really like it.
   - b) and I really liked it.

7. I did that report
8. I've done that report
   - a) sometime last week.
   - b) so I'll put it on your desk today.

9. I never met Carol;
10. I've never met Carol;
    - a) I hope I have the chance to.
    - b) I wish I'd had the chance to.

11. Ever thought of going to Scotland;
12. Did you think of going to Scotland
    - a) it's really nice, you know?
    - b) when you had your holiday in Europe?

C Write *present perfect* or *past simple* in the correct sentences.

Example:
When the action has an effect now or in the future you use the ___present perfect.___

1. When you want to begin a conversation on a new subject without mentioning a definite time you often use _____

2. When you are talking about a definite finished time in the past you use _____

3. When both an action and its results are finished you normally use _____

4. When you are talking about people who are dead you normally use _____

5. When you are talking about experiences in the lives of living people, without mentioning a definite time, you often use _____

Present perfect and past simple 2

Look at the pictures and complete what each of the people is saying. Use a verb from the box in the correct form. (You need to use some verbs twice.)

| forget   have   break   go   spill   put   ski   draw   hit   drive   be   land |

1. Ouch! _____ my head!

2. Drat! I _____ my wine!

3. I _____ to Australia in 1982.

4. Oh dear! _____ the phone number!

5. In 1969, they _____ on the moon.

6. Ouch! I think _____ my leg!

7. Mrs Thatcher _____ Prime Minister from 1979 to 1990.

8. This is the first time I _____ since my driving test!

9. I'm afraid I _____ before!

10. She _____ five kittens.

11. Palaeolithic people _____ these pictures.

12. I'm sure I _____ it under the pillow.

56 Relative clauses 1
defining relative clauses

A You are explaining to a foreign friend how to get to your house. Complete the instructions using the words in the box.

> launderette   pelican crossing   chemist   (traffic lights)
> playground   newsagent   shop assistant

Come out of the station and turn left. You'll come to some lights that tell the cars to stop and go, which are called **traffic lights**. Turn right. Go past a 1 _____ (a shop that sells medicines), and a place where you get your clothes washed, a 2 _____. Take the next left. You pass a place where children play, called a 3 _____, and then you cross the road at the 4 _____, which says if it's safe to cross. Take the next right, past a shop that sells newspapers, called a 5 _____, and my house is the red one without a number. If you can't find it, ask the 6 _____, that's the person who works in the shop.

B Put a tick ✓ in the box if the relative clause(s) can be used to end the sentences correctly and a cross ✗ if it is not possible.

Example: A florist is someone
 a) that sells flowers. ✓
 b) who sells flowers. ✓
 c) sells flowers. ✗

1 A church is a place
 a) you pray in. ☐
 b) you pray. ☐
 c) where you pray. ☐

2 A rose garden is a garden
 a) where you grow roses. ☐
 b) you grow roses. ☐
 c) where roses grow. ☐

3 An orphan is someone
 a) who parents have died. ☐
 b) whose parents have died. ☐
 c) of whose parents have died. ☐

4 A washing machine is a machine
 a) who washes clothes. ☐
 b) which/that washes clothes. ☐
 c) you wash clothes in. ☐

5 A penguin is a kind of bird
 a) who can't fly. ☐
 b) which/that can't fly. ☐
 c) you can't fly. ☐

C Finish these sentences with relative clauses using the words in brackets. Where a relative clause is possible with or without a relative pronoun (*who, where, why, when, which, whose*), give both alternatives.

Example: A widow is someone (die)
 a) **whose husband has died.**

1 Birthdays are times (celebrate)
 a) _____
 b) _____

2 Strangers are people (not know)
 a) _____
 b) _____

3 An alarm clock is a clock (wake up)
 a) _____

4 A vegetarian is someone (not eat)
 a) _____

5 A playground is a place (play)
 a) _____
 b) _____

6 A bachelor is a man (not marry)
 a) _____

7 Making money is the reason (work)
 a) _____
 b) _____

Relative clauses 2
defining and non-defining relative clauses

Peter Wright had a strange experience last year and wrote it down. Now he wants to add some more information to it. Add the extra information using relative clauses with *which*, *who*, *where* and *when*.

I went back to Fordham Green, <u>where I was born and brought up,</u> with an old friend called Melanie Dyson. We stopped at the church _____ _____ because I wanted to walk down the road to the house _____.

This was the first time I had been back since 1979 _____.

I was feeling very emotional _____ _____ so I wasn't too surprised to see the figure of old Hilda Greenway sitting on a chair outside her old cottage. I stopped and said hello. She said hello, and then she just started telling me that my father didn't like the new motorway _____ _____ and _____ _____. I didn't know anything about it of course, and I just didn't think about the fact that she was still alive although she must have been at least a hundred years old, if not more.

Well, anyway, just then Melanie _____ _____ came up and asked me what I was doing. I turned towards her and said, 'Let me introduce you to Hilda,' and turned back again, but there was no one there. Hilda had disappeared.

I didn't know what to think. I described what had happened and what Hilda had said; and then how old she must have been _____. Melanie _____ didn't tell me I was mad; instead she took me to the doctor's house _____ and I repeated everything I had seen and heard.

Apparently Hilda had died twenty years before, at the age of eighty, but they really were building a motorway going past the village _____ _____ so I believe I really did speak to the spirit of Hilda Greenway _____.

Speech bubbles:
- I was born and brought up there.
- 1 It's the first building in the village.
- 2 I had spent my childhood there.
- 3 This is when my father died.
- 4 This wasn't surprising in the circumstances.
- 5 The council was building it past the village.
- 6 It was going to go through his favourite wood.
- 7 She had parked the car and walked back.
- 8 This is when I realised how crazy the whole thing was.
- 9 I trust her completely.
- 10 She had passed it on her way down.
- 11 It really would go through my father's favourite wood.
- 12 This is why I am opposing the plan to build it.

Relative clauses 3
defining and non-defining relative clauses

A Read the sentences and decide which statement, *a* or *b*, describes the defining relative clause and which describes the non-defining relative clause. Note that where there is a comma (,) in writing there is a pause in speech.

Defining relative clauses

Non-defining relative clauses

Example:
Lambs *that are born early* are given special care. _a_

Lambs, *which are young sheep*, are usually born in spring. _b_

The relative clause tells you:	a) which particular group of lambs she is talking about. b) more about lambs in general, ie what lambs are.

1 Now I'm going to swallow the sword *that my assistant, Julia, is holding*. _____

2 Now I'm going to swallow the sword, *which my assistant, Julia, is holding*. _____

The relative clause tells you:	a) more about the situation, ie where the sword is. b) which sword he is talking about.

3 Miners *who work underground all their lives* usually have health problems. _____

4 Miners, *who work underground*, usually have health problems. _____

The relative clause tells you:	a) which group of miners have health problems. b) more about miners in general; ie why they have health problems.

5 The London *I knew 20 years ago* has gone forever. _____

6 London, *which I knew 20 years ago*, has changed forever. _____

The relative clause tells you:	a) more about the situation, ie she used to know London. b) which particular London she means, ie the one she knew 20 years ago.

B Complete these sentences by writing *defining* or *non-defining* in each space.

1 You use a _____ relative clause to tell your listener which one, or which particular group, you are talking about.
2 You use a _____ relative clause to add extra information to your sentence; it does not usually help to identify which one/group you are talking about.
3 You do not use a comma in writing, or pause in speech, before a _____ relative clause.
4 You do use a comma, or pause in speech, before a _____ relative clause.
5 You can use *that* in a _____ relative clause.
6 You cannot use *that* in a _____ relative clause.
7 You can omit *who*, *which* and *that* if it is the object of a _____ relative clause.
8 You cannot omit *who*, *which* or *that* in a _____ relative clause.

Relative clauses 4

mixed relative clauses

59

A Complete the sentence on the left with the correct relative clause, *a* or *b*.

1 King James I's Bible ___ is still a best-seller in its revised version.
2 He wrote most of his books in Latin, and the only one ___ was *The Temple*.

a) , which was produced in English in 1611,
b) that was produced in English before 1611

3 The assistant ___ was Jane Carr!
4 The customer ___ was Chris Greaves!

a) you served
b) who served you

5 The detective ___ has just been suspended from the police.
6 The burglar, Joe Truman ___ has just escaped from prison again.

a) , whom we arrested 5 years ago,
b) who arrested us 5 years ago

7 That's not the thing ___
8 He didn't understand what she said ___

a) , which annoyed her.
b) that annoyed her.

9 That's Madha Jones ___ on the wall.
10 That's Madha Jones ___ is on the wall.

a) , whose painting, *The Party*,
b) , who's painting *The Party*

11 I'd like to introduce you to a person ___
12 I'd like to introduce you to Mary ___

a) , who I've known since birth.
b) I've known since birth.

B Use the words in the pictures to write a relative clause in each sentence.

Example:

That's Admiral Nelson, <u>who fought at the Battle of Trafalgar.</u>

1 There were three apples _____

2 That's the woman _____

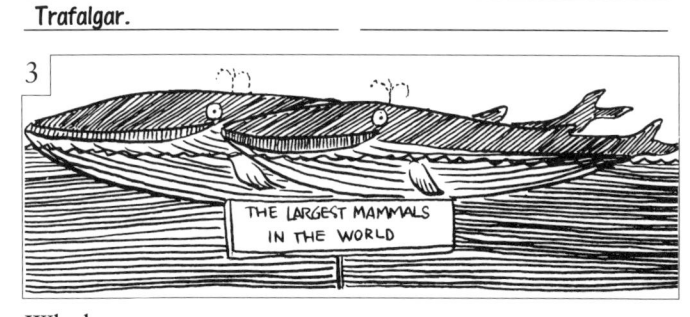

3 Whales _____ seem to have a complex language.

4 This is the person _____.
Everyone admired her.

60 Reporting 1

A Use a verb from the box to complete the report about each picture.

> (ask) warn suggest invite order insist remind tell

Example:
She _asked_ the hairdresser _to cut her hair very short._

1 He _____ the tourists _____
2 She _____ the dog _____
3 The waiter _____ the customer _____
4 She _____ the boy _____
5 He _____ his girlfriend _____
6 He _____ his daughter _____
7 The manager _____ her secretary _____

B Maria is staying with a British family. Report what they say to her.

- Would you like to have dinner with us?
- Why don't you have an early night?
- Don't forget to change some money.
- Don't hit your head on the bathroom shelf.

1 They _____ dinner with them.
2 They _____ an early night.
3 They _____ some money.
4 They _____ the bathroom shelf.

PHOTOCOPIABLE

© Will Forsyth, Sue Lavender 1995. Published by Heinemann English Language Teaching. This sheet may be photocopied and used within the class.

Reporting 2

A Humphrey is a manager at a publishing company. He needs to appoint a new assistant. Put each of the verbs from the box into its correct sentence.

> (advised) agreed thought wanted asked insisted
> said suggested told persuaded reminded

1 Humphrey __advised__ the company to appoint a new assistant.
_____
_____
_____
_____
_____

2 Humphrey _____ the company should appoint a new assistant.
_____
_____
_____

B Choose the correct verb each time

1 Humphrey *suggested/advised* them to put an advert in the local paper.
2 Humphrey *said/told* the candidates should come for an interview.
3 Humphrey *persuaded/insisted* the company to offer a good salary.
4 Humphrey *wanted/thought* his new assistant should do some of his work.
5 Humphrey *agreed/asked* his assistant should have a permanent contract.

C Complete Humphrey's report on some of the interview questions he asked the candidates. Use a word or phrase from each box in each question.

if what	previous experience they had they had taken their last job university course they had liked	previous experience they had they had taken their last job a university course had been

I asked them _____ . I asked them _____ .
I asked them _____ . I asked them _____ .
I asked them _____ . I asked them _____ .

D Here is Humphrey's report. Correct any of his sentences which are incorrect.

Example: I invited several candidates should come for an interview. __candidates to come__

1 I asked them to tell me why they wanted the job. _____
2 I asked them have you worked for a publishing company before. _____
3 I asked what had been their previous job. _____
4 I also wanted to know what will they do in the future. _____
5 I advised some candidates should come back when they had more experience.
_____
6 I said the best two to come back for a second interview. _____
7 I suggested the company to raise the salary. _____
8 I told the company which person I had chosen. _____

62 Simple and continuous 1
senses and actions

A Put each verb in the correct space.

| feel | hear | listen | look | see | touch |

1. 'You'll have to _____ if you want to _____ it.'

2. 'If you _____ now, you'll _____ my favourite part.'

3. 'If you _____ the speaker, you can _____ the music!'

B Read the questions and complete the answers using a verb from the box. Be careful; sometimes you have to use:

- can/could   (for example, I can feel/I could feel)
- am/was -ing   (for example, I'm feeling/I was feeling)
- present or past simple   (for example, I feel/I felt)

| feel | smell | taste | hear/listen to | see/look at |

Example:
Why did that man open ten bottles of wine and then only drink a little of each one?
(He/it) **He was tasting it.**

1. Don't eat that; it's for the guests!
   (Don't worry, I/only/it) _____
2. What's in this ice cream?
   (I don't know, but I/honey and nuts) _____
3. How do you know the letter's from his girlfriend?
   (It/of perfume) _____
4. Why are you holding your nose up like that?
   (I/this wonderful sea air) _____
5. How do you know there was someone next door?
   (I/voices, but they've stopped now) _____
6. Why don't you talk to me?
   (Please be quiet, I/the music) _____
7. Do you know someone called Lara Sharman?
   (Yes, in fact I/her tomorrow) _____
8. Do you think she'll come?
   (Yes. In fact I/her coming now; look) _____
9. Why did you stop?
   (I/that church; it's really beautiful) _____
10. What's wrong? You're shaking.
    (I/really cold) _____
11. Why have you got your hand in the water?
    (I/the temperature) _____
12. What's that? Is it an earthquake?
    (I/not/anything) _____

Simple and continuous 2
senses and actions

63

A Match each sentence with one of the two pictures.

1 He's seeing the president.
2 He can see the president.

3 I can taste coconut.
4 I was tasting the coconut.

5 I could hear music.
6 I was listening to music.

7 I can smell perfume.
8 I'm smelling the perfume.

B Write the numbers of the sentences from part A in the correct sentence.

1 Sentences _1_, ____, ____ and ____ describe *actions*.
2 Sentences ____, ____, ____ and ____ describe *feelings* or *senses*.

C Choose the correct ending to each sentence, *a* or *b*.

1 'What's the matter?'   a) 'I thought I saw something move out there.'
                          b) 'I thought I looked at something move out there.'

2 He sat in front of the picture for 20 minutes;   a) he was seeing it.
                                                    b) he was looking at it.

3 If it's something you feel or sense, you usually say   a) 'I can taste/feel/smell it.'
                                                          b) 'I'm tasting/feeling/smelling it.'

4 If it's an action, you usually say   a) 'I can taste/feel/smell it.'
                                        b) 'I'm tasting/feeling/smelling it.'

5 *See* and *hear* are usually   a) senses.
                                  b) actions.

6 *Look* and *listen* are   a) senses.
                             b) actions.

64 Simple and continuous 3
states and actions

In the year AD 79 in Italy, the volcano Vesuvius erupted. The lava and ash covered the town nearby, which is called Pompeii. It was very sudden and many people were killed where they stood. Here is one of the houses in Pompeii as it is now.

Look at the pictures and complete the sentences in the past using the verbs in boxes.

| stand   keep   (be)   look |

This __was__ the house of the Gaius family. It 1 _____ alone in what was a beautiful position. The walls were painted and 2 _____ very bright then. The Gaius family was rich and 3 _____ nine servants.

| be   have   weigh   hold |

Marcus Gaius 4 _____ a swim when the volcano erupted. He was a fat man, and probably 5 _____ nearly 142 kg. The bath 6 _____ cleaned by two servants. It 7 _____ 355 000 litres of water.

| taste   make   weigh   keep |

A servant 8 _____ a fish for the next day. The cook 9 _____ a fish sauce, a Pompeiian speciality. The sauce 10 _____ strong and salty; it was very popular. Another servant 11 _____ the family's dinner hot.

| stand   have   have   hold   look   taste |

The Gaius family 12 _____ dinner. A servant 13 _____ a plate of meat for one of the family and another servant 14 _____ the food to check that it was all right for the family to eat. The master of the house, Julius, 15 _____ up at the time. He 16 _____ out of the window; perhaps he knew what was happening. We will never know what expression he 17 _____ on his face.

© Will Forsyth, Sue Lavender 1995. Published by Heinemann English Language Teaching. This sheet may be photocopied and used within the class.

> # Simple and continuous 4
states and actions

A Match each sentence with the correct picture, *a* or *b*.

1 The machine shows you what he thinks.
2 The machine shows you what he's thinking.

3 'Do you have espresso coffee?'
4 'Are you having espresso coffee?'

5 'He's being funny.'
6 'He's funny.'

7 It's holding four people.
8 It holds four people.

9 It weighs four kilos.
10 She's weighing four kilos.

B Match the meanings on the left with the sentences on the right.

What you mean	What you say
1 You want to know someone's opinion.	a) What are you thinking?
2 You want to know why someone is quiet.	b) What do you think?
3 You possess a shower.	a) I have (got) a shower.
4 You are in the shower.	b) I'm having a shower.
5 He is a funny person.	a) He's being funny.
6 His actions at the moment are funny because he wants to make people laugh.	b) He's funny.
7 It has four people in its hands.	a) It's holding four people.
8 It is big enough for four people.	b) It holds four people.

© Will Forsyth, Sue Lavender 1995. Published by Heinemann English Language Teaching. This sheet may be photocopied and used within the class.

PHOTOCOPIABLE

So and such 1

A Complete the sentences with *so* or *such*.

I went to Spain last year and I enjoyed it __so__ much that I want to go back. I had 1 ____ beautiful weather that I stayed outdoors all the time and the sea was 2 ____ warm that I never wanted to get out. The shops were selling 3 ____ wonderful cheap leather that I bought presents for all my friends. The people I met were 4 ____ friendly – they were always inviting me to their homes. I did 5 ____ many interesting things I can't even remember them all.

B Ferhan is visiting England. It is very different from her own country. Complete the sentences with phrases using *so* or *such* and the opposite of the word in *italics*.

Example: She thinks the city is *boring* because she comes __from such an interesting city.__

1 She thinks the weather is *cold* because in her country it's _____
_____
2 She thinks the house is *small* because she has _____
3 She thinks there's very *little* to do here because in her own city there's
_____
4 She thinks the people drive *well* because the people in her own country
_____
5 She thinks English families are *small* because she has _____
6 She thinks they have *short* names because in her country everyone's name is
_____
7 She thinks the food is *bad* because they have _____
8 She thinks there are very *few* children in the streets because in her country there _____

C Write out these thoughts in complete sentences, using *so* or *such* before the word(s) in *italics* each time. Do not change the order of words given.

Example: wind *strong* – nearly   __The wind was so strong that it nearly blew__
blew bike over   __my bike over.__

1 *dark* night – couldn't see
  path in front of me
2 then saw crowd of people;
  many – couldn't count them
3 they were all glowing with
  bright light – lit the path ahead
4 I going *fast* – couldn't stop

5 but suddenly vanished; I
  never *scared* – in life before

So and such 2

A Read these sentences and put the phrases in *italics* into the correct box.

Noun phrases, a lot, a few, a little	Adjectives, adverbs, much, many, few, little
such a kind man	

Example:
What I like about Peter is that he's *such a kind man*.

1 What I like about Peter is that he's *so kind*.
2 It was *so cold* that I didn't go out.
3 He was *so good* at mathematics that he went to university when he was 16 years old.
4 There are *such a lot of people* here that we'll never find him.
5 I've never tasted *such delicious fruit* as I did in Singapore.
6 They drove away *so fast* that no one could catch them.
7 Thank you for giving me *so much* of your time.
8 He was *such a little boy* when he was 10 that everyone thought he was younger.
9 They're *such interesting people* that it's strange they have *so few* friends.

B Decide whether these sentences are correct. Put a tick ✓ in the box if the sentence is right and a cross ✗ if it is not. Correct the sentences with mistakes.

1 I've never met anyone such interesting before. ☐ _____
2 Italy is so beautiful country that I never want to live anywhere else. ☐ _____
3 There was so little food that everyone still felt hungry after the meal. ☐ _____
4 I met so nice man last weekend. ☐ _____
5 I've never eaten so nice food before. ☐ _____

C Complete the sentences below by using *so* or *such* and an adjective from the box below each time. Note that you may also need to add *a* or *an*.

| rough   ancient   reserved   many |

1 There were _____ people at the concert that it was impossible to find you.
2 We never really got to know her because she was _____ person.
3 The sea was _____ that we couldn't set sail.
4 The carvings were _____ that no one remembered who had made them.

68 Subject and object questions 1

A Here is part of a leaflet about a new film 'Murder at Midnight'. Unfortunately, the leaflet has been torn and part is missing. Complete the questions you need to ask to find out the missing information about the new film.

MURDER AT MIDNIGHT – COMING SOON

Starring Martin Symes as
Directed by
Produced by
Filmed on location in
Musical score by

Novel by
This film has won
'Time Out' says
Opens in London on

Example:
Who __does Martin Symes__ star as?
1 Who _____ the film?
2 Who _____ the film?
3 Where _____ filmed?
4 Who _____ the musical score?
5 Who _____ the novel?
6 What _____ the film won?
7 What _____ say?
8 When _____ in London?

B Here is a review of the film 'Murder at Midnight'.

> MURDER AT MIDNIGHT: based on the popular Detective Clithero novel by A J Smith
> One night, the butler discovered the body of Lord Mayhew in his study. He had been mysteriously poisoned by wine. The following day, the butler saw a strange figure, then the butler too was attacked ...
> All is solved by Detective Clithero. This is a film you MUST see!

Make questions to the answers using the words in the box.

What Who	did –	the butler find? the butler see? poisoned Lord Mayhew? solved the crime? wrote the novel?

Example: __What did the butler find__ ?   Lord Mayhew's body.
1 _____ ?   The wine.
2 _____ ?   A strange figure.
3 _____ ?   Detective Clithero.
4 _____ ?   A J Smith.

Subject and object questions 2

A Match each question with the correct picture, *a* or *b*.

1 How many plates broke?
2 How many plates did they break?

3 What crashed into you?
4 What did you crash into?

5 'Who did you invite?'
6 'Who invited you?'

B Decide which question, *a* or *b*, the statements refer to.

a) Who taught Einstein?
b) Who did Einstein teach?

1 *Who* refers to the teacher. _____
2 *Who* refers to the pupils. _____
3 *Who* is the subject of the verb teach. _____
4 *Who* is the object of the verb teach. _____

a) What did the discovery lead to?
b) What led to the discovery?

5 *What* refers to the cause of the discovery. _____
6 *What* refers to the result of the discovery. _____
7 *What* is the subject of the verb lead. _____
8 *What* is the object of the verb lead. _____

C Megan teaches in a primary school. Here are some answers the children in her class have given her. Use the verb in bold to write the question Megan asked them.

Example: Columbus **discovered** America.   Who _discovered America_ ?

1 Shakespeare **wrote** Hamlet.   Who _____ ?
2 The Americans **landed** on the moon in 1969.   Who _____ ?
3 Light **travels** at 300 000 km per second.   How fast _____ ?
4 The phone was **invented** by Bell.   Who _____ ?
5 Canada and Mexico **border** the USA.   Which countries _____ ?
6 Wren **designed** St Paul's Cathedral.   Who _____ ?
7 The moon **causes** the sea level to change.   What _____ ?
8 Neil Armstrong **said**, 'One small step for a man, one giant step for mankind'.   What _____ ?

70 Substitution words 1

A Match the beginning of each phrase or sentence on the left with *a* or *b* on the right.

1 Those sandwiches are great;   a) have it.
2 This is the last sandwich;   b) have one.

3 He doesn't like them.   a) She doesn't like either of them.
4 Which one does she like?   b) She doesn't like them either.

5 Have you won the $1 million prize?   a) I hope so.
6 Will you go to prison?   b) I hope not.

B Your friend, Mariana, has just arrived to stay with you in your flat. She asks you some questions. Complete your replies to her questions using the verb given, in the correct form, and one of the words from the box.

> so   myself   that   one
> them   not   this   any   it
> (yourself)   some   to

Mariana's questions | **Your replies**

Example:
Can I make some coffee? | No need to ask. Just **help yourself!** (help)

1 Do you have any milk? | Sorry, I don't think I _____ (have got)

2 Where's the nearest shop? | Don't worry about the shops. I'm sure my neighbour _____ (lend)

3 By the way, do you feel like watching a video tonight? | I'm afraid I'm feeling rather tired so I don't really _____ (want)

4 Well, how about watching it tomorrow instead? | Sounds fine; I _____ (prefer)

5 Do you think you'll be late back from work tomorrow? | Well, I _____ (hope)

6 And are you free on Friday evening? | I'll have to check, but I _____ (think)

7 In that case, why not give Sam and Ella a ring? | OK. I'll try not to forget to _____ (phone)

8 Do you still have their number? | No, I don't. I think I must _____ (lose)

9 Do you need some paper to write it on? | That's OK, thanks. I can just _____ (use)

10 I saw your book. Are you learning French? | Well, I haven't got very far, but I'm trying to _____ (teach)

11 One last thing, could I read your newspaper? | Sorry, but I've been so busy that I _____ (not buy)

© Will Forsyth, Sue Lavender 1995. Published by Heinemann English Language Teaching. This sheet may be photocopied and used within the class.

Substitution words 2

71

A This is part of a conversation between two people. Decide which replies are possible. In each case, one is *not* possible.

Example:
- **A:** How did you enjoy the party?
- **B:** a) I enjoyed it very much. ✓
  b) I enjoyed very much. ✗
  c) I enjoyed myself very much. ✓

1 A: Would you like to see a film tonight?
  B: a) I think I'll be busy. ☐
  b) I don't think. ☐
  c) I don't think so. ☐

2 A: Oh, why's that?
  B: a) I have to meet someone. ☐
  b) I have to meet someone else. ☐
  c) I have to meet other person. ☐

3 A: Could I see you for just a short time?
  B: a) I'm afraid not; I won't have time. ☐
  b) I'm afraid no; I won't have time. ☐
  c) I'm afraid I won't have time. ☐

4 A: Would you like to watch TV tomorrow?
  B: a) Yes, I would. ☐
  b) Yes, I'd like. ☐
  c) Yes, I'd like to. ☐

5 A: OK, see you tomorrow then.
  B: a) Yes, I hope it. ☐
  b) Yes, I hope so. ☐
  c) Yes, I hope to. ☐

6 A: Shall I order you a pizza?
  B: a) Yes, I'd like that. ☐
  b) Yes, I'd like one. ☐
  c) Yes, I'd like it. ☐

7 A: And what about beer?
  B: a) Yes, get some. ☐
  b) Yes, get them. ☐
  c) Yes, get one. ☐

B Use the pictures to finish what the people are saying. Include a word from the box.

| some   so   one   myself |

1 It should fit me; at least I _____

2 This is delicious rice. Why don't you _____ ?

3 I'm having a beer. Are you sure you won't _____ ?

4 This camera has a special timer so I can take photos _____

C Answer the question by putting each phrase into the correct space, *A* or *B*.

| I hope   He'd like   I'm afraid   I think   He wants   He said   I asked him   He'd love |

'Is he arriving tomorrow?'	
A: '_____ so/not.'	B: '_____ to.'
_____ _____	_____ _____
_____ _____	_____ _____

© Will Forsyth, Sue Lavender 1995. Published by Heinemann English Language Teaching. This sheet may be photocopied and used within the class.

PHOTOCOPIABLE

72

Used to 1
used to do and *get used to doing*

A Match each sentence with the correct picture: *a, b* or *c*.

1 She used to cycle up the hill.
2 She's used to cycling up the hill.
3 She's getting used to cycling up the hill.

4 He's used to changing her nappies.
5 He used to change her nappies.
6 He's getting used to changing her nappies.

B Answer the questions explaining that there is or was a problem. Use the correct form of *used to* in every answer.

The problem

Example:
'How's your new bicycle?' — 'It's great now that **I've got used to the new handlebars.**'   The new handlebars were strange at first.

1 'How's England? Are you enjoying it?' — 'I will if I can _____'   You don't like driving on the left.

2 'How's the new house?' — 'It's OK, but I ____ never _____'   You have a tiny kitchen.

3 'Are you enjoying your stay in Sweden?' — 'Yes, but I can't _____'   You don't like the cold!

4 'You know London very well, don't you?' — 'Not any more, but I _____'   You knew it well before it changed.

5 'Do you like living in Cornwall?' — 'It's very nice now that Sarah _____'   Sarah didn't like her new school at first.

6 'I hear you've gone back to university. How is it?' — 'I'm enjoying the life, but after all this time I _____'   You haven't studied for years.

7 'Do you think you'll enjoy your new job?' — 'I'm not sure; I _____'   You have never given people orders before.

8 'Do you play much sport?' — 'Not now, but I _____'   You played football before your accident.

9 'How's the new job going?' — 'I'm enjoying it, but I ____ still _____'   You have never got up so early before.

© Will Forsyth, Sue Lavender 1995. Published by Heinemann English Language Teaching. This sheet may be photocopied and used within the class.

PHOTOCOPIABLE

Used to 2

used to do and *get used to doing*

73

A Match the beginning of each sentence with its ending, *a* or *b*.

1 I'm used to driving on the left
2 I used to drive on the left

a) when I lived in England several years ago.
b) because I've been in England for two years now.

3 I was used to cycling to work
4 I used to cycle to work

a) because I did it every day.
b) but I use the car all the time these days.

5 I used to go to bed late
6 I'm used to going to bed late

a) and I can always get up early the next day.
b) but I haven't got enough energy these days.

7 I was used to living in a small house
8 I got used to living in a small house

a) because I'd never lived in a big one.
b) when I was living in Japan.

9 I got used to the cold
10 I'm used to the cold

a) after I'd been here for a few months.
b) because I come from Siberia.

11 I used to have an open fire a long time ago
12 I'm used to an open fire

a) but I'll have to get used to it again living here.
b) because I've got used to it living here.

B Match each expression on the left with its correct meaning on the right.

1 *I used to do it* means
2 *I was used to it* means
3 *I am used to it* means
4 *I'll get used to it* means
5 *I've got used to it* means

a) this is normal for me.
b) this was normal for me.
c) I did this regularly, but I don't any more.
d) I wasn't used to it at first, but now I am.
e) I'm not used to it now, but I will be.

C Match each sentence beginning on the left with its correct ending on the right.

1 I used to
2 I'm used to
3 I got used to
4 I'll get used to

a) rice every day; I come from Taiwan.
b) eat rice every day but now I eat pasta mostly.
c) eating rice every day when I go to live in China next year.
d) eating rice every day when I lived in Japan last year.

D Make as many combinations as possible using one item from each box each time. There is a maximum of five possible combinations.

used to +	infinitive	(for example, *use* a computer)
be used to +	verb -ing	(for example, *using* a computer)
get used to +	noun	(for example, *computers*)

1 _____
2 _____
3 _____
4 _____
5 _____

74 Wish 1
wish + could, simple past and past perfect

A Read the picture story and complete John's thoughts below each picture. Use the verb in brackets in the correct tense.

1. John went fishing one day in March. When he started it had been a beautiful day, but not any more.

I wish I **had listened** (listen) to the weather forecast before I left.

2. Also, he hadn't checked to see if there was enough petrol for the engine.

Oh no. I wish I _____ (check) the petrol.

3. It started to rain, and John got very wet because he didn't have any waterproof clothes.

I wish I _____ (have) some waterproofs.

4. He didn't have a compass with him either, so he didn't know where he was …

I'd be able to get home if I _____ (bring) a compass.

5. Fortunately, a few hours later a ship came into view,

I hope they _____ (see) me.

6. and rescued him.

If they _____ (not come) I might have died out here.

B Maggie's wishes have changed since she was a child. Use each verb twice to complete both of Maggie's sentences with the correct form of the verb in brackets. For example (see): *I saw/didn't see, I could see/couldn't see* or *I had seen/hadn't seen*.

When I was a child, *I wished* …   but now *I wish* …
Example:
(live)   I *lived* in a skyscraper,   I *didn't live* in a flat.
(leave)   1 I _____ school earlier,   2 I _____ so soon.
(live)   3 I _____ by myself,   4 I _____ alone.
(start)   5 I _____ smoking,   6 I _____ smoking.
(watch)   7 I _____ TV all day,   8 I _____ so much.

Wish 2

wish + simple past, past perfect, *would*

A Joachim, aged 4, is staying with his grandmother. He arrived about a week ago. In some ways she is finding his visit rather difficult. Look at some of the problems and then complete what she says using the verb in *italics*. Write each wish in the correct sentence.

Problems

He *misses* his parents.
He doesn't *put* his toys away.
He *plays* with his food.
He doesn't *do* what I say.
When he arrived, he *said* he didn't want to stay!
He doesn't *like* vegetables.
He can't *dress* himself.
On Monday, he *hit* the dog!
Last week, he *broke* a very expensive vase.

1 Yes, we had several problems with Joachim last week:
Example: I wish ___he hadn't hit the dog.___
  I wish _____
  I wish _____

2 Sometimes I think he really could behave much better if he tried; for example,
Example: I wish ___he would put his toys away.___
  I wish _____
  I wish _____

3 But, of course, I know he's only a child so there are lots of things that won't change until he grows up, but still ...
Example: I wish ___he liked vegetables.___
  I wish _____
  I wish _____

B Now look at his grandmother's thoughts and complete what she says to Joachim using the verb in *italics*.

Thoughts

Example: You *scratched* my car.   I wish ___you hadn't scratched my car.___
1 You don't *play* by yourself.   I wish _____
2 You've *lost* your favourite toy.   I wish _____
3 You can't *read*.   I wish _____
4 You *sing* at 6.00 every morning.   I wish _____
5 I *shouted* at you last week.   I wish _____
6 Yesterday, you *tore* my favourite book.   I wish _____
7 You *chase* the dog.   I wish _____
8 You *haven't* any other children to play with.   I wish _____
9 You *aren't* old enough to understand how difficult you are.   I wish _____

© Will Forsyth, Sue Lavender 1995. Published by Heinemann English Language Teaching. This sheet may be photocopied and used within the class.

Wish 3
states and actions

A Match the picture, *a* or *b*, with the wish.

1 I wish you could speak to me.
2 I wish you would speak to me.

3 I wish you would buy me a walkman.
4 I wish you had bought me a walkman.

5 I wish you would get your hair cut.
6 I wish you had shorter hair.

B Match each wish with the most appropriate ending, *a* or *b*.

7 I wish it didn't rain so much in England
8 I wish it hadn't rained so much in England

a) then we could have seen much more.
b) then we could spend our holiday there.

9 I wish you would listen to me;
10 I wish you had listened to me;

a) I could help you so much.
b) I could have helped you so much.

C Use the wishes in parts A and B to answer the questions.

1 Which of the wishes can be re-written in the form 'Please … !'?
   __2__ Please __speak to me__ !   ____ Please _____!
   ____ Please _____!   ____ Please _____!
2 Which of the wishes refer only to the past? __4__ ____ ____
3 Which of the wishes refer to a dream about changing something in the present? __1__ ____ ____

D Match the description with the correct form.

1 To talk about something in the past which you can't change now you use
2 To make a request for change in the future or to talk about possible future change you use
3 To express a dream about changing something which exists you use

a) wish + simple past
   (I wish you did X)
b) wish + past perfect
   (I wish you had done X)
c) wish + would
   (I wish you would do X)

Review 1

Jan has just married Gwyneth and has gone to live with her in Wales. Here is a letter he has written to his friend, Dan. He has made 23 mistakes in his letter. Write the letter in your exercise book and correct the mistakes. The number of mistakes in each paragraph is written at the bottom of the page.

```
Dear Dan,
```

1   I'm writing to thank you for a wonderful present you gave us for our wedding. Today I'm at home because I lost my voice; in fact, I don't think I can speak again for the next two or three days. This gives me plenty of time to write letters!

2   We arrived to Cardiff just a week after the wedding. I like already Wales very much. Many people here want to know what are the differences between Wales and Denmark, but I don't think there are so a lot. One of the most impressive, perhaps, is the beautiful view of sea and mountains which I am seeing from our window. Of course, the language is also very different! Although my English has improved quite a lot I'm still afraid of make mistakes. As for Welsh, I don't think I'll never manage to understand it!

3   I haven't already found a job, but it's very important for me to find one soon as I can't settle in here unless I don't find one. I don't want to depend of Gwyn for ever! In fact, I had my first interview the other day. The interviewer was very interested to hear I was an import-export manager in a Danish company and all the reasons why I had left …

4   I also had a bad experience the other day. The roads here are such empty that I got into my car and completely forgot which way to drive! Eventually a policeman has stopped me and told me I had better be driving on the left. He warned me I could prosecute. He told me to report to the police station next week. Some of my friends say I have to pay a fine when I go.

5   By the way, what did happen to you after the wedding? I rang your hotel, but they told me you already left. Anyway, please let us know when can you visit. Gwyneth sends her love,

Yours,
Jan

6   P.S. I can't remember if you took any photos at the wedding so I'm enclosing a picture in this letter if you didn't.

Paragraph   1 – 3 mistakes   3 – 4 mistakes   5 – 3 mistakes
            2 – 7 mistakes   4 – 5 mistakes   6 – 1 mistake

Review 2

Jan has married Gwyneth and is living in Wales. This is his second letter to his friend, Dan. He has made 23 mistakes in his letter. Write the letter in your exercise book and correct the mistakes. The number of mistakes in each paragraph is written at the bottom of the page.

```
Dear Dan,
```

1   Thank you so much for writing back such quickly. I'm afraid I still haven't managed to find a job, but I hope to get it soon. Fortunately, the person lives next door to us is interested in learning Danish so I am able to earn a little money.

2   Because Gwyneth is out all day I sometimes feel a little lonely. I really wish she wouldn't need to work so much. When I feel lonely I often can't stop to think about about my friends and family in Denmark, and I just remember to eat my favourite Danish food and all the other things I used do at home. Occasionally, I wish I didn't come here because I'm sure if we had stayed there Gwyneth could find a job by now. But anyway, I'm enjoying here on the whole although I'm still not used to hear the language.

3   I really like countryside round here and yesterday, because I had plenty of spare time, I could go for a long walk through the hills. I was frightened of getting lost, but eventually I could get home without too many problems.

4   I spend most of my time thinking about finding a work. Denise, the woman who husband I'm teaching Danish, has given me some good advices. She has suggested me to put an advert in the local newspaper. I really wish I found a good job. The local school needs an economics teacher, but economics aren't really my field.

5   Yes, I'd love you to come and visit as soon as possible. I hope that by the time you get here I have found a job. I'd like to ring you but I don't have your number any more - I think perhaps I would have left it in Denmark but I'm not sure. Is it possible for you to phone me? If so, please ring in the evening because I'll probably look for a job during the day-time.

Yours

Jan

6   P.S. Please remember getting in touch as soon as you can. Gwyneth asked me to remember to send you her love too.

Paragraph   1 – 3 mistakes   3 – 3 mistakes   5 – 2 mistakes
            2 – 8 mistakes   4 – 6 mistakes   6 – 1 mistake

Review 3

A Ka Man is visiting New Zealand. Here are some sentences from a letter she has written to an English-speaking friend in her home, Hong Kong. Match the beginning of each sentence with its correct ending.

1. Ever since I arrived here
2. But when I first arrived
3. Being here really makes me
4. This is the first time
5. I can't get used to
6. I'm not really looking forward
7. New Zealand is one of the most interesting places
8. If only I had more time
9. I know my family would like me
10. But I really don't want to think

a) expressing myself only in English.
b) I've ever seen.
c) I could stay much longer.
d) I didn't know anyone.
e) I've been to an English-speaking country.
f) to going back home.
g) to come home soon.
h) feel so happy.
i) of leaving this place.
j) I've been speaking English all the time.

B Complete what the speaker in each picture is saying.

1. Is this the first time you _____?

2. I can't get used to _____.

3. I expect you're looking forward _____.

4. This is one of the most exciting things _____.

5. I'm trying to make him _____.

6. Would you like _____?

Review 4

Match the beginning of each sentence with its correct ending, *a* or *b*.

1	With one book between two, there are just	a)	plenty.
2	With one book for everyone and three spare, there are	b)	enough.
3	Do you happen to know where	a)	Sally is?
4	I've looked everywhere; where	b)	is Sally?
5	It depends	a)	on what he said.
6	I'm thinking	b)	of what he said.
7	Are you seeing	a)	what I mean?
8	Do you see	b)	Francesca this evening?
9	What do you think	a)	of doing this evening?
10	What are you thinking	b)	of the government?
11	The bomb exploded	a)	suddenly.
12	The bombs were exploding	b)	all day.
13	I didn't want to go swimming because	a)	I was swimming that morning.
14	I hurt my leg when	b)	I had been swimming that morning.
15	I'll be going to the shops	a)	so if you want something I can get it.
16	I'll go to the shops	b)	if you tell me what you want.
17	It looks like	a)	extremely painful.
18	It looks	b)	an extremely painful cut.
19	They said they will	a)	arrive early yesterday.
20	They said they would	b)	arrive early tomorrow.
21	It sounds as if	a)	there's a really bad storm outside.
22	It sounds	b)	really stormy outside.
23	She can't have left yet;	a)	it's getting late.
24	She could have left by now;	b)	it's much too early.
25	I've got one film and a documentary on video –	a)	would you like to watch a film?
26	I've joined a video club –	b)	would you like to watch the film?
27	If you ask what caused the accident,	a)	I'd say a wet road.
28	If you ask what the accident caused,	b)	I'd say severe injuries.
29	We stayed until the end of the concert although	a)	it not being very good.
30	We stayed until the end of the concert despite	b)	it wasn't very good.
31	Music	a)	is an important part of education.
32	The music	b)	is much too loud.
33	She said she hated coconut	a)	until she tasted my Coconut Supreme.
34	She said she'd hated coconut	b)	so I didn't give her any.

Review 5

Here are some common signs and notices. Complete each sign by choosing the correct word or words.

Example: If you *didn't use/aren't used* to strenuous exercise consult your doctor first.

1 **These leaflets are free. Please take *it/one*.**

2 **The police *is/are* to be informed if the alarm sounds.**

3 Your life-jacket is under *the/a* seat.

4 DENTAL CARE: Please remember *telling/to tell* your dentist if you are taking any form of medicine.

5 This medicine *should/had better* be taken three times daily.

6 We always try *answering/to answer* your call as soon as possible.

7 Bake for 45 minutes or until the top looks *like brown/brown*.

8 All visitors *should/could* report to reception.

9 If you wish you *would be/were* in the sun right now, give us a ring on 086 5416311 for the winter holiday of a lifetime!

10 *Who did do it?/Who did it?* Murder in Madrid – a detective thriller.

11 When you complete our course you *can/will be able to* take perfect photos.

12 No classes *will be taught/will teach* over the New Year holiday.

13 If you can't read this sign it *can be/could be* time for you to see your optician.

14 Please put *litter/the litter* in the bin.

15 *Plenty of/Enough* seats still available.

16 **This *could/must* have happened to you! Be careful! Fireworks are dangerous.**

17 This bus *carries/is carrying* 44 passengers.

18 This plant comes from *Ecuador that/Ecuador, which* is on the equator.

19 Danger! This product *will explode/will be exploding* on contact with water.

20 Bridge closed *because/because of* road repairs.

Answer Key

2 Adverbs of time 1
A
1 I haven't read it yet.
2 I still haven't rung her.
3 had it since I went to India.
4 've ever met him.
5 already read it.
6 've never been to an Indian restaurant.
7 've had it for six months.
8 ever thought of buying a computer?

B
1 yet
2 still
3 already

3 Adverbs of time 2
A
1 I have already been to Australia.
2 I haven't been to Australia yet.
3 Have you ever been to Australia?
4 I've never been to Australia.
5 I still haven't been to Australia.
6 Australia is the most beautiful country I've ever seen.

B
1 c   2 f   3 d   4 e   5 g   6 a

C
1 It's the most beautiful picture I've ever seen.
2 I haven't ever been to Germany but I'd like to go one day.
3 You were talking about going to Munich; have you been there yet?
4 I'm trying to find someone who knows about Canada; have you ever been there?
5 Although Mongolia has opened its borders it's still difficult to fly there.
6 We haven't visited Padua yet, but we plan to go in the spring.

4 Adverbs of time 3
A
1 often   5 just   9 already
2 since   6 sometimes   10 until
3 twice   7 before   11 rarely
4 ago   8 once   12 yet
Hidden word: occasionally

B
1 just now
2 long ago
3 never ever

5 Adverbs of time 4
A
1 ago   6 yet
2 when   7 for
3 since   8 while
4 never   9 still
5 ever
Hidden word: The trainer

B
1 over   7 whenever
2 ago   8 ages
3 long   9 these days
4 moment   10 time
5 sooner or later   11 present
6 every now and then 12 during

6 Advice and suggestions 1
A
1 Why don't you rent a car?
2 I think you'd better rent a car.
3 How about visiting Wales?
4 If I were you I'd rent a car.
5 You could always rent a car.
6 Have you thought of staying in a bed and breakfast?
7 Why not rent a car?
8 Perhaps you ought to come and stay with me.

B
1 of using a bicycle?
2 buy a CD player?
3 to have an eye test/to have your eyes tested.
4 look (them up) in a dictionary.
5 you take a tent?
6 having fish?
7 borrow my coat.

7 Advice and suggestions 2
A
1 a   2 b   3 b   4 a   5 b   6 b

B
a)   2 b   6 b
b)   3 b   4 a   5 b
c)   3 b   5 b
d)   2 b   4 a

8 Articles 1
A
1 a violent film   5 the violence   9 films
2 violent films   6 the quality   10 children
3 Violence   7 the film
4 life   8 a film

B
1 c   2 a   3 b
4 a   5 c   6 b

C
Unemployment is one of the most important problems in the world today. It affects all countries: not only South America, Africa and Asia, but also Europe and the United States too. And it is not just a modern problem either; it has been with us for centuries. Unemployment destroys people's lives, it breaks up the family and it makes society poor. The question is: what can we do about it?

9 Articles 2
A
The true sentences are: 2, 3, 5, 6

B
a 5   b 6   c 3   d 2

C
1 b   2 a   3 a   4 b   5 b   6 a
7 a   8 b

10 Articles and countable and uncountable nouns
1 If you need help, please ask for assistance
2 Advice Centre
3 Roadworks ahead
4 Collect your luggage here
5 Will all personnel please report to the main office.
6 English spoken here.
7 Please shut the door
8 Travel agent
9 The sun rises in the east and sets in the west

10 Please leave cameras at the desk
11 Please turn off the light.
12 If you have a complaint, please ask to see the manager.
13 Foreign money not accepted
14 The End
15 Please ring the bell for service
16 Take a card; any card

11 Countable and uncountable 1
1 time
2 times
3 glass
4 a glass
5 glasses
6 lights
7 a light
8 light
9 hope
10 a hope
11 hopes
12 lambs
13 a lamb
14 lamb
15 experiences
16 experience
17 an experience
18 beliefs
19 a belief
20 belief

12 Countable and uncountable 2
A
1 a 2 b 3 b 4 a 5 a 6 b 7 a 8 b

B
1 c) i) hairs   2 a) iv) a hair   3 d) ii) hair

13 Countable and uncountable 3
A
uncountable
2 countryside
3 accommodation
5 secrecy
6 advice
8 travel
9 furniture
11 information
12 work

countable
1 teeth
4 mice
7 sheep
10 people

B
always singular
the news
each (of them)
politics
either (of them)
everyone
maths

always plural
the police
scissors
the poor
both (of them)
all (of them)
trousers

C
2 a beauty   3 a difficulty
4 an experience   7 an icecream
10 a talk

14 Enough and plenty
A
1 b   2 a

B
1 just the right amount
2 there aren't quite enough
3 there isn't enough
4 there are plenty
5 there aren't enough
6 just the right number
7 there isn't enough
8 this isn't big enough
9 these aren't big enough
10 there is plenty
11 there are far too many

15 Futures 1
A
1 will have completed
2 will have taken
3 will be talking
4 will be typing
5 will have left
6 will be shining
7 will have left
8 will have declined
9 will have fallen

B
1 will have moved
2 will be selling
3 will have installed
4 will have appointed
5 will have raised
6 will have solved
7 will be printing

16 Futures 2
A
1 b   2 a   3 b   4 b   5 a   6 b

B
Actions in progress
… 'll be living in a warmer climate.
… 'll be working as an agriculturalist.
… 'll be living in a comfortable house.

Actions completed
… 'll have met the right person.
… 'll have paid back all the money my parents lent me.
… 'll have published the results of my research thesis.

C
1 will have doubled
2 will be feeding
3 will have found
4 will be facing
5 will have contributed

17 Futures 3
1 Actually, I'm meeting an old friend there.
2 Not long, I'm/'ll be leaving on Sunday.
3 Yes, I'm going to visit the colleges.
4 In that case, I'll go there too.
5 I'm afraid I'll be working (in the university library) at three o'clock.
6 Let's see. Shall I ring you at 6.00 pm on Thursday?
7 In that case, I think I'll buy one.
8 If it's good, shall I get you one?
9 OK. I'll ring you on Thursday.

18 If sentences 1
A
1 b   2 a

B
1 hadn't gone to America
2 caught the 10 o'clock bus
3 had had a gun
4 had thrown the receipt away
5 didn't study hard
6 had told
7 had come in
8 hadn't invented
9 had stopped

19 If sentences 2
A
Clauses that are possibly true: 3, 4, 7, 8
Clauses that are definitely not true: 1, 2, 5, 6, 9

B
1 c   2 a   3 b

C
1 If the captain sent a radio signal before the ship sank
2 If Les is here now
3 If Les had been here now
4 If Sarah said anything to your boss while you were away
5 If Sarah had said anything to your boss while you were away
6 If Ali bought the tickets when the box office first opened
7 If Ali had bought the tickets when the box office first opened
8 If I'd had any more food
9 If I have any more food

20 If sentences 3
1 If I had had some change I would have rung.
2 Don't worry. If I need anything I'll help myself.
3 I wouldn't have brought them if I hadn't wanted to.
4 I'll certainly come if I have time.
5 Don't worry. If I don't remember I'll ring you to ask again/I can always ring if I can't remember.
6 Well, I think I would (like to) go there if I had enough money.
7 I'm not sure. She'll come if she (has) got a plane ticket.
8 Yes, I'd still be/have been waiting if I hadn't caught it.
9 I would go to bed if I weren't/wasn't waiting for a phone call.

21 Indirect questions 1
A
1 a family day excursion ticket to London is/costs?
2 if you have a double room available this weekend./if a double room is available this weekend.
3 it costs to hire a car for two days.
4 flight BA 272 arrives?
5 if you are open on Sunday evenings?/if the restaurant is open on Sunday evenings?
6 you can come and meet the Dumals on Sunday?/you would like to come and meet them on Sunday?

B
1 what time, ?   4 how long, .
2 whether, ?   5 How much, ?
3 if, ?   6 what, ?

22 Indirect questions 2
A
1 e), c), a)   2 d), b)
B
1 ✓   2 ✗   3 ✓
C
1 Do you happen to know what time the next bus is due?
2 no change
3 Oh, do you happen to know where the Comsoft Computer shop is?

23 Infinitive and gerund 1
1 to listen   6 to tell
2 coming   7 shouting
3 marrying   8 to feed
4 to watch   9 coming
5 throwing   10 to go

24 Infinitive and gerund 2
A
1 a   2 b

B
1 to light   4 to teach   7 going
2 lighting   5 to lock   8 to tell
3 teaching   6 going

C
1 b   2 a   3 a   4 b   5 b   6 a
7 b   8 a   9 a   10 b   11 a   12 b

25 Infinitive and gerund 3
A
1 a   2 a   3 b   4 b   5 a   6 a
7 b

B
1 remembered, saw   4 told, regretted
2 saw, stopped   5 regretted, told
3 stopped, saw

C
1 a   2 b   3 b   4 a

26 Infinitive and gerund 4
A
1 arrange   7 manage
2 avoid   8 miss
3 choose   9 plan
4 consider   10 practise
5 decide   11 refuse
6 deny   12 recall

B
1 to stay   8 seeing
2 to get   9 dropping
3 to have   10 to visit
4 to meet   11 sitting
5 stealing   12 speaking
6 attacking   13 to go
7 to give

27 Linking words 1
A
1 b   2 c   3 a   4 d

B
1 … unless you want to see the sights.
2 … in case you get lost.
3 … although many people think they are too crowded.
4 … unless you want to spend a lot of money.
5 … as long as you arrive early to avoid the crowds.
6 … although you will find it very noisy.
7 … as long as you don't mind a long journey.
8 … in case you want to buy a lot of presents.

28 Linking words 2
A
1 despite
2 Due
3 because
4 Although
5 spite
6 However

B
1 e   2 d   3 c   4 g   5 a   6 h
7 h   8 b

29 Linking words 3
A
1 b   2 a   3 a
4 c   5 a   6 b
7 b   8 a   9 c
10 b   11 c   12 a

B
1 Due to the train strike, we took the car.
2 Despite the fact that I was hungry, I couldn't eat the snails.
3 Although the weather was rough, the boat set sail.
4 The government resigned because the economy collapsed.
5 They said the bridge wouldn't last, but it is still standing.
6 Take my phone number in case you need it.

C
... I'm writing in case you ever decide to go to Ireland. Despite the bad weather, I had a wonderful time. Although I didn't have much money, it was still easy to find places to stay, and in spite of having been to Ireland twice before, I still found plenty of new things to see. Due to it being an island, the weather can be quite changeable. It's a pity that because I didn't have/of not having much free time I couldn't stay longer ...

30 Look, look like, look as if 1
A
1 She looks
2 She looks as if
3 She looks
4 She looks as if
5 She looks like
6 She looks like
7 She looks
8 She looks as if

B
1 sounds like
2 She sounds as if
3 She sounds like
4 She sounds as if
5 She sounds
6 She sounds as if
7 She sounds like
8 She sounds

31 Look, look like, look as if 2
A
1 d ice
2 f (old) socks
3 b applause/clapping
4 e runner
5 a old woman

B
1 like
2 like
3 —
4 as if/as though

C
1 smells like 3 sounds like 5 looks as if/as though
2 tastes 4 sounds as if/as though

32 Modal verbs 1
1 Could/Would
2 could/might
3 could
4 would
5 should/could
6 could
7 could/might
8 would

33 Modal verbs 2
A
1 a   2 b   3 b   4 a   5 b   6 a
7 a   8 b   9 b   10 a

B
a 7   b 8   c 3   d 4   e 10   f 5
g 6   h 9

C
1 should
2 could, might
3 should
4 could
5 could
6 would
7 would
8 could, might

34 Modal verbs 3
A
1 Will you have to find a job there?
2 Will you have to learn Spanish while you're there?
3 Will you be able to go camping in the countryside?
4 Will I/we be able to write to you?
5 Will you be able to drive a car there?
6 Will you have to have lots of injections?
7 Will you be able to come home if you really want to?

B
1 do you have to be/must you be
2 can vote/will be able to vote
3 will have to start
4 won't be able to go
5 won't have to pay
6 must keep/have to keep
7 can do/will be able to do
8 will have to see

35 Modal verbs 4
A
1 won't be able to
2 can't

B
1 a ✗ b ✓   4 a ✗ b ✓
2 a ✗ b ✓   5 a ✓ b ✓
3 a ✓ b ✓

C
1 b   2 a   3 c   4 d

36 Modal verbs 5
A
1 could/might even have died
2 should have listened
3 should have checked
4 shouldn't go
5 could/might easily have missed
6 would have been
7 would know
8 could learn/would learn
9 should have taken
10 should have told
11 shouldn't have gone out
12 would have been
13 should have known
14 could/might still catch

B
1 would have done it.
2 shouldn't have bought them.
3 couldn't have stolen it.
4 might/could have taken it/the plane.
5 should have rung her.

37 Modal verbs 6
A
2 have gone
3 have lent
4 find/have found
5 have finished
6 have fallen/fall
7 have grown
8 have looked
9 have stopped

B
1 would have been
2 could/might have finished
3 should have dug
4 would certainly have finished
5 would/might/could have fallen
6 should have finished
7 could move

38 Modal verbs 7
A
1 b   2 a   3 b   4 a   5 a   6 b
7 a   8 b

B
1 b   2 a   3 a   4 b   5 a   6 b

C
Possible endings: 1 b   2 a   3 a, b   4 a, b
5 a   6 a   7 b

39 Modal verbs 8
A
1 b, d, g, k 2 e, h, j 3 a, c, f, i

B
1 b 2 a 3 d 4 e 5 c 6 h
7 f 8 g 9 j 10 i 11 k

40 Modal verbs 9
A
1 a) might/could   c) will
  b) won't   d) might/could
2 a) could/might   c) can't
  b) could/might   d) must
3 a) can't havehave c) might have/could
  b) might have/could have d) must have
4 a) must have have c) could have/might
  b) can't have have d) could have/might

B
1 could, might   5 must have
2 must   6 can't have, couldn't have
3 can't, couldn't   7 could have, might have
4 could, might

41 Modal verbs 10
A
1 heard/could hear   6 climbed
2 couldn't phone   7 couldn't start
3 decided   8 found
4 could swim/swam   9 began
5 managed to swim   10 managed to row

B
1 b 2 b 3 b 4 a

42 Modal verbs 11
A
1 b 2 a 3 b 4 a 5 a 6 b
7 a 8 b

B
3 is not correct.

C
1 correct   2 ... she managed to cycle ...
3 correct   4 correct
5 correct   6 ... she could cycle ...

43 Passives 1
2 I'm afraid it's been stolen.
3 I'm afraid it's going to be demolished.
4 I'm afraid it's been burgled.
5 I'm afraid it'll be enlarged.
6 I'm afraid it's being diverted.
7 I'm afraid it's been knocked down.
8 I'm afraid it's thrown away.
9 I'm afraid it hasn't been built yet.
10 I'm afraid she's being interviewed.

44 Passives 2
A
1 b 2 a 3 a 4 b 5 a 6 b
7 b 8 a

B
1 a 2 b 3 b 4 a 5 b 6 a
7 b 8 a 9 a 10 b

45 Passives 3
A
1 a 2 a 3 b

B
1 They stole $500 000
2 they are painted
3 she was examined (by a doctor)

46 Passives 4
A
4 It (the film)   7 The film
5 Ms O'Neill's costumes   8 It (the film)
6 Her dresses

B
4 It was directed by Luca Lopez and produced by Pablo Mendes.
5 Ms O'Neill's costumes are said to be outstanding.
6 Her dresses were specially designed by Gocci.
7 The film has already been nominated for several awards.
8 —

C
1 pasta   5 China   9 Italy
2 Italy   6 He   10 it
3 Marco Polo 7 discovery   11 Italy
4 it   8 pasta   12 China

47 Past and present
A
1 did you notice
2 are you shaving
3 have you been waiting
4 have you done
5 were you driving
6 do you meet

B
1 was living
2 realised
3 had been
4 was climbing
5 saw
6 had been drawn
7 was
8 recognised
9 was
10 began
11 have been haunting/have haunted
12 used to sacrifice/sacrificed

48 Pasts 1
1 had driven/   17 wasn't
  had been driving   18 had
2 could   19 came
3 got   20 was waiting
4 checked   21 didn't look
5 had not returned   22 saw
6 went   23 had told
7 went   24 gave
8 heard   25 drank
9 wondered   26 felt
10 had followed   27 fell
11 waited   28 killed
12 was   29 said
13 left   30 wasn't
14 was   31 had confessed
15 had gone   32 had hidden
16 slipped

49 Pasts 2
A
1 b 2 a 3 a 4 b 5 b 6 a
7 a 8 b 9 a 10 b

B
1 they had been driving   3 had worked
2 had been deserted   4 died

C
1 same   3 different
2 different 4 same

D
1 b   2 a

50 Pasts 3
1 was carrying, died
2 gave, promised
3 were going to see, heard
4 was wearing, saw
5 was going to send, died
6 told, had written
7 took, met
8 sent, had been killed

51 Pasts 4
A
1 were climbing (a hill).
2 had just got up.
3 were eating (a picnic).
4 was going to have a shower.
5 finished.

B
a 2   b 1 and 3   c 5   d 4

52 Prepositions 1
A
1 for   4 to   7 in   10 of
2 to   5 in   8 at
3 of   6 in   9 from
Hidden word: information

B
1 I can depend on
2 remember people by name
3 never criticise you behind your back
4 disagree with me sometimes, but not always
5 take advantage of other people
6 need to have a reason for everything
7 frequently get out of control
8 can't take pleasure in simple things
9 laugh at other people's misfortunes

53 Prepositions 2
A
2 on   5 in
3 through   6 with
4 with

B
1 you (drink) through
2 you (find) words in
3 you (keep) money in
4 you (borrow) books from
5 you (hang) coats on
6 you (open) bottles with
7 you (play) with
8 you (look) through
9 you (keep) money in
10 you (keep) keys on

54 Present perfect and past simple 1
A
1 b   2 a   3 b   4 a

B
1 b   2 a   3 a   4 b   5 b   6 a
7 a   8 b   9 b   10 a   11 a   12 b

C
1 present perfect   4 past simple
2 past simple   5 present perfect
3 past simple

55 Present perfect and past simple 2
1 Ouch! I've hit my head.
2 Drat! I've spilt my wine.
3 I went to Australia in 1982.
4 Oh dear! I've forgotten the phone number!
5 In 1969 they landed on the moon.
6 Ouch! I think I've broken my leg!
7 Margaret Thatcher was Prime Minister from 1979 to 1990.
8 This is the first time I've driven since my driving test.
9 I'm afraid I haven't skied before!
10 She's had five kittens.
11 Palaeolithic people drew these pictures.
12 I'm sure I put it under the pillow.

56 Relative clauses 1
A
1 chemist   4 pelican crossing
2 launderette   5 newsagent
3 playground   6 shop assistant

B
1 a✓ b✗ c✓   3 a✗ b✓ c✗   5 a✗ b✓ c✗
2 a✓ b✗ c✓   4 a✗ b✓ c✓

C
1 a) when/which you celebrate
  b) you celebrate
2 a) you don't know
  b) who you don't know
3 a) which wakes you up
  b) that wakes you up
4 a) who doesn't eat meat
5 a) where children play
  b) children play in
6 a) who isn't married
7 a) you work
  b) why you work

57 Relative clauses 2
1 , which is the first building in the village,
2 where/in which I had spent my childhood
3 , (which is) when my father died
4 which wasn't surprising in the circumstances,
5 (which) the council was building past the village
6 which was going to go through his favourite wood
7 , who had parked the car and walked back,
8 , which is when I realised how crazy the whole thing was
9 , who/whom I trust completely,
10 , which she had passed on her way down,
11 , which really would go through my father's favourite wood,
12 , which is why I am opposing the plan to build it

58 Relative clauses 3
A
1 b   2 a   3 a   4 b   5 b   6 a

B
1 defining   5 defining
2 non-defining   6 non-defining
3 defining   7 defining
4 non-defining   8 non-defining

59 Relative clauses 4
A
1 a   2 b   3 b   4 a   5 b   6 a
7 b   8 a   9 b   10 a   11 b   12 a

B
1 (that/which) she couldn't reach.
2 whose name she can never remember.
3 , (which are) the largest mammals in the world,
4 (whom) I was talking about.

60 Reporting 1
A
1 He insisted the tourists should visit Yorkshire.
2 She ordered the dog to sit.
3 The waiter suggested the customer should have fish.
4 She warned the boy to be careful.
5 He invited his girlfriend to go to a party.
6 He told his daughter to tidy her room.
7 The manager reminded her secretary to ring Ms Adams.

B
1 They invited Maria to have dinner with them.
2 They suggested that she should have an early night.
3 They reminded her to change some money.
4 They warned her not to hit her head on the bathroom shelf.

61 Reporting 2
A
1 wanted, asked, told, persuaded, reminded
2 agreed, thought, insisted, said, suggested

B
1 advised   4 thought
2 said   5 agreed
3 persuaded

C
what previous experience they had
if they had previous experience
if they had taken a university course
what their last job had been
what university course they had taken
if they had liked their last job

D
1 correct
2 I asked them if they had worked for a publishing company before.
3 I asked what their previous job had been.
4 I also wanted to know what they would do in the future.
5 I advised some candidates to come back when they had more experience.
6 I asked/told the best two to come back for a second interview.
7 I suggested the compnay should raise the salary.
8 correct

62 Simple and continuous 1
A
1 look, see
2 listen, hear
3 touch, feel

B
1 Don't worry; I'm/I was only tasting it.
2 I don't know, but I can taste honey and nuts.
3 It smells of perfume.
4 I'm smelling this wonderful sea air.
5 I heard/I could hear voices but they've stopped now.
6 Please be quiet, I'm listening to the music.
7 Yes, in fact I'm seeing her tomorrow.
8 Yes, in fact I can see her coming now; look.
9 I was looking at that church; it's really beautiful.
10 I feel really cold.
11 I'm feeling the temperature.
12 I didn't/don't/can't/couldn't feel anything.

63 Simple and continuous 2
A
1 b   2 a   3 a   4 b   5 a   6 b
7 b   8 a

B
1 3, 5, 6   2 1, 2, 4, 7

C
1 a   2 b   3 a   4 b   5 a   6 b

64 Simple and continuous 3
1 stood   10 tasted
2 looked   11 was keeping
3 kept   12 was having
4 was having   13 was holding
5 weighed   14 was tasting
6 was being   15 was standing
7 held   16 was looking
8 was weighing   17 had
9 was making

65 Simple and continuous 4
A
1 b   2 a   3 b   4 a   5 a   6 b
7 a   8 b   9 b   10 a

B
1 b   2 a   3 a   4 b   5 b   6 a
7 a   8 b

66 So and such 1
A
1 such   2 so   3 such   4 so   5 so

B
1 so warm/hot   5 such a big/large family
2 such a big/large house   6 so long
3 such a lot/so much   7 such good food
4 drive so badly   8 are so many

C
1 It was such a dark night that I couldn't see the path in front of me.
2 Then I saw a crowd of people; there were so many that I couldn't count them.
3 They were all glowing with such a bright light that it lit the path ahead.
4 I was going so fast that I couldn't stop.
5 But suddenly they vanished/But they suddenly vanished; I have never been so scared in my life before.

67 So and such 2
A
Noun phrases
4 such a lot of people   8 such a little boy
5 such delicious fruit   9 such interesting people

Adjectives and adverbs
1 so kind   3 so good   7 so much
2 so cold   6 so fast   9 so few

B
1 ✗ anyone so interesting/such an interesting person
2 ✗ so beautiful that/such a beautiful country
3 ✓
4 ✗ such a nice man
5 ✗ such nice food

C
1 so many
2 such a reserved
3 so rough
4 so ancient

88

68 Subject and object questions 1

A
1 directed
2 produced
3 was it
4 wrote
5 wrote
6 has
7 does 'Time Out'
8 does it/the film open

B
1 What poisoned Lord Mayhew?
2 Who did the butler see?
3 Who solved the crime?
4 Who wrote the novel?

69 Subject and object questions 2

A
1 a 2 b 3 b 4 a 5 b 6 a

B
1 a 2 b 3 a 4 b 5 b 6 a
7 b 8 a

C
1 Who wrote *Hamlet*?
2 Who landed on the moon in 1969?
3 How fast does light travel?
4 Who invented the phone?
5 Which countries border the USA?
6 Who designed St Paul's Cathedral?
7 What causes the sea level to change?
8 What did Neil Armstrong say?

70 Substitution words 1

A
1 b 2 a 3 b 4 a 5 a 6 b

B
1 've got any
2 will/could lend us/you some
3 want to
4 'd prefer that
5 hope not
6 think so
7 phone them
8 have lost it
9 use this
10 teach myself
11 haven't bought one/didn't buy one

71 Substitution words 2

A
1 a ✓ b ✗ c ✓   4 a ✓ b ✗ c ✓   6 a ✓ b ✓ c ✗
2 a ✓ b ✓ c ✗   5 a ✗ b ✓ c ✓   7 a ✓ b ✗ c ✓
3 a ✓ b ✗ a ✓

B
1 hope so   2 have some   3 have one
4 of myself

C

A	B
I hope	He'd like
I'm afraid	He wants
I think	I asked him
He said	He'd love

72 Used to 1

A
1 c 2 b 3 a 4 b 5 c 6 a

B
1 … I can get used to driving on the left.
2 … I'll never get used to having a tiny kitchen.
3 … I can't get used to the cold.
4 … I used to know it well before it changed.
5 … Sarah has got used to/is used to her new school.
6 … I'm not used to/I can't get used to studying.
7 … I'm not used to giving people orders.
8 … I used to play football (before my accident).
9 … I still haven't got used/but I'm still not used to getting up so early.

73 Used to 2

A
1 b 2 a 3 a 4 b 5 b 6 a
7 a 8 b 9 a 10 b 11 a 12 b

B
1 c 2 b 3 a 4 e 5 d

C
1 b 2 a 3 d 4 c

D
used to   + infinitive
be used to   + verb-ing
be used to   + noun
get used to   + verb-ing
get used to   + noun

74 Wish 1

A
1 had checked   4 see/will see/have seen
2 had   5 hadn't come
3 had brought

B
1 could leave   5 could start
2 hadn't left   6 hadn't started
3 lived   7 could watch
4 didn't live   8 hadn't watched

75 Wish 2

A
1 he hadn't said he didn't want to stay.
  he hadn't broken a very expensive vase.
2 he wouldn't play with his food.
  he would do what I say.
3 he didn't miss his parents.
  he could dress himself.

B
1 you would play by yourself.
2 you hadn't lost your favourite toy.
3 you could read.
4 you wouldn't sing at 6.00 every morning.
5 I hadn't shouted at you last week.
6 you hadn't torn my favourite book.
7 you wouldn't chase the dog.
8 you had some other children to play with.
9 you were old enough to understand how difficult you are.

76 Wish 3

A
1 a 2 b 3 b 4 a 5 b 6 a

B
7 b 8 a 9 a 10 b

C
1 3 Please buy me a walkman!
   5 Please get your hair cut!
   9 Please listen to me!
2 8, 10
3 6, 7

D
1 b 2 c 3 a

Review 1

Paragraph 1:
1 for the wonderful present
2 because I've lost my voice
3 I'll be able to speak

Paragraph 2:
4 in Cardiff
5 I already like Wales
6 what the differences are
7 such a lot/so many
8 which I can see
9 afraid of making
10 I'll ever manage

Paragraph 3:
11 I haven't found a job yet
12 unless I do find one
13 depend on Gwyn
14 I had been an import-export

Paragraph 4:
15 are so empty
16 a policeman stopped me
17 I should be driving
18 I could be prosecuted
19 I will have to pay

Paragraph 5:
20 what happened to you
21 you had already left
22 when you can visit

Paragraph 6:
23 in case you didn't

Review 2

1 ... writing back so quickly.
... I hope to get one soon.
... the person who lives ...
2 ... I really wish she didn't need to work so much.
... I often can't stop thinking ...
... I just remember eating ...
... I used to do at home.
... I wish I hadn't come here ...
... Gwyneth could have found a job ...
... I'm enjoying myself here on the whole ...
... I'm still not used to hearing the language.
3 I really like the countryside ...
... I went for a long walk ...
... eventually I got home ...
4 ... finding a job./finding work.
... the woman whose husband ...
... some good advice.
She has suggested that I put ...
I really wish I could find ...
... economics isn't really my field.
5 ... perhaps I have left it in Denmark/perhaps I left it in Denmark ...
I'll probably be looking for a job ...
6 Please remember to get in touch ...

Review 3

A
1 j 2 d 3 h 4 e 5 a
6 f 7 b 8 c 9 g 10 i

B
(suggestions)
1 have flown
2 working without a calculator/not using a calculator
3 to having a (cold) drink
4 I will have ever done
5 jump through the hoop
6 me to open the door for you

Review 4

1 b	2 a	17 b	18 a
3 a	4 b	19 b	20 a
5 a	6 b	21 a	22 b
7 b	8 a	23 b	24 a
9 b	10 a	25 b	26 a
11 a	12 b	27 a	28 b
13 b	14 a	29 b	30 a
15 a	16 b	31 a	32 b
		33 b	34 a

Review 5

1 one
2 are
3 the
4 to tell
5 should
6 to answer
7 brown
8 should
9 were
10 Who did it?
11 will be able to
12 will be taught
13 could be
14 litter
15 Plenty of
16 could
17 carries
18 Ecuador
19 will explode
20 because of

Index

a   8, 10, 11, 13
ability   32, 34, 41, 42, Review 5
able to   34, 41, 42, Review 5
active   *see* passive and active
adjectives   66
adverbs of frequency   4
adverbs of time   2, 3, 4, 5
advice   6, 7, Review 2
advise   60
after   48
ago   4, 5
agree   60
already   2, 3, 4, 5,
   Review 1
although   27, 28, 29, Review 4
any (pronoun)   70
articles   8, 9, 10, 13, Review 2, Review 4
ask   60
as long as   27

be able to   *see* able to
because   28, 29
before   4, 74
be going to   *see* going to
be used to   *see* used to

can and able to   34, 41
can with sense verbs   62
conditional sentences   *see* 'if' sentences
continuous tenses   *see* simple and continuous tenses
could   32, 36, 37, Review 5
could, able to and manage   41, 42
could for deduction   39, 40
could after wish   75
countable and uncountable   10, 11, 12, 13,
   Review 1, Review 2

deduction   39
defining relative clauses   *see* relative clauses
despite   28, 29, Review 4
do, does and did in questions   47
due to   28, 29
during   4, 5
dynamic verbs   *see* stative and dynamic

else   70
enough, plenty and too   14, Review 1, Review 4,
   Review 5
ever   2, 3, 4, 5

feel   62
for and since   2, 5
future continuous   15, 16, 17
future perfect   15, 16
future progressive   *see* future continuous
future (the)   15, 16, 17, Review 5
future (the) of modal verbs   34, 37

gerund   *see* infinitive and gerund
get used to   *see* used to
going to   17

have to   34
had better   6
how/what about -ing   6
however   28, 29

if, if only   74
   if and whether in indirect questions   21
   'if' sentences (conditionals)   18, 19, 20,
      Review 4
   if I were you   6
in case   27
in spite of   28, 29

indirect commands and questions   21, 22,
   Review 4
infinitive and gerund   23, 24, 25, 26, Review 1,
   Review 3, Review 5
insist   60, 61
invite   60, 61

just   4

like and as if   30, 31, Review 4, Review 5
linking words   27, 28, 29
   see also although, as long as, because, despite,
   due to, in case, in spite of, therefore, unless
look and see   62
look like/as if   30, 31, Review 4, Review 5

managed to   41, 42
many   66
might   32, 36, 37, 39, 40
modal verb   32, 33, 34, 35, 36, 37, 38, 39, 40,
   41, 42
   see also can, could, future (the) of modal verbs,
   have to, might, ought to, past (the) of modal
   verbs, shall, should, will, would
much and many   66
must   39, 40, Review 5
must and will have to   34

never   2, 4, 5, Review 1
not   70
now   4
nowadays   5

object and subject questions   68, 69, Review 5
often   4
one (pronoun)   70
ought to   6

passive and active   43, 44, 45, 46
past and present   47
past (the)   48, 50,
   Review 4
past (the) of modals   36
past continuous   48, 49, 50, 64, Review 4
past perfect   48, 49, 50
past perfect in 'if' clauses   18, 19
past perfect in indirect
   speech   60, 61
past perfect after wish
   74, 75
past progressive *see* past continuous
past simple   47, 48, 49, 50, 54, 55, 62, 63, 64,
   65
past simple in 'if' sentences   18, 19
past simple in indirect speech   60, 61
past simple after wish   74, 75
persuade   60, 61
plenty, enough and too   14, Review 1, Review 4,
   Review 5
plural   *see* singular and plural
prepositions   52, 53
present and past   47
present perfect   47, 54, 55
present simple   62, 63, 64, 65
progressive tenses   *see* continuous tenses

questions   21, 22, 47, 60, 61, 68, 69
   see also indirect questions; subject and object
   questions

relative clauses
   defining   56, 57, 58, 59, Review 2
   non-defining   57, 58, 59, Review 2
relative pronouns   *see* relative clauses, that,
   where, which, who, whose

regret to do, doing   23, 24, 25
remember to do, doing   23, 24, 25, Review 2
remind   60
reporting in indirect speech   60, 61, Review 4

see and look   30, 60, 62
sense verbs and actions   62, 63, 64, 65
shall   17
should   6, 32, 36, 37, Review 5
simple present   *see* present simple
simple past   *see* past simple
simple and continuous tenses   47, 62, 63, 64, 65, Review 2, Review 4, Review 5
since and for   2, 4, 5
singular and plural   10, 11, 12, 13
smell like/as if   30
so   66, 67, 70
some and any   70
sometimes   4
sound like/as if   30
stative and dynamic   62, 63, 64, 65
still   2, 3, 4, 5
stop to do/doing   23, 24
subject and object questions   68, 69, Review 5
substitution words   70
such   66, 67, Review 1
suggest   6, 60, 61, Review 2

taste like/as if   30, 62
tell   60, 61
tenses   *see* future continuous, future perfect, future, past continuous, past perfect, past simple, present perfect, present simple, simple and continuous tenses, stative and dynamic
that, pronoun in relative clauses   56, 57, 58, 59
the   8, 9, 10, 11, 12, 13
therefore   28, 29
think   60
too, enough and plenty   14, Review 1, Review 4
try to do/doing   23, 24

uncountable   *see* countable and uncountable
unless   27
until   4, 48
used to and be/get used to   72, 73, Review 2, Review 3
usually   4

want   60, 61
warn   60, 61
what/how about?   6, 7
where (in relative clauses)   56, 57
whether (in reported questions)   21
which (in relative clauses)   56, 57, 59
while   4
who (in relative clauses)   57, 59, Review 2
whom (in relative clauses)   59
whose (in relative clauses)   56, 59
'wh' questions   68, 69
why don't you?   6, 7
will   15, 17, 39
will in 'if' sentences   18, 19, 20
wish   66, 74, 75, 76, Review 2
would   32, 36, 37, 75, Review 2
would in 'if' sentences   18, 19, 20
would after wish   75
word order in questions   68, 69

yet   2, 3, 4, 5, Review 4

Questionnaire

At Heinemann ELT we are committed to continuing research into materials development. We would be very interested to hear your feedback about this photocopiable resource book:

- Have you enjoyed using *Grammar Activities* 2?
- What features did you like most?
- What did you like least?
- Do you have any suggestions for improvements?
- What other kinds of materials would you like to see in a photocopiable format?

We would also welcome your comments, queries or suggestions on other supplementary or coursebook materials. Please send them to:

The Editor,
Heinemann Teacher Resources,
Heinemann ELT,
Halley Court,
Jordan Hill,
Oxford OX2 8EJ,
UK.

If you prefer to send a fax, please send to +44 865 314193.

Thank you for your help.